Jeannette Chau

UPSIZING IN A DOWNSIZING WORLD

Lessons learned and tips to get you back on your feet after job loss

iUniverse, Inc.
Bloomington

Upsizing in a Downsizing World
Lessons learned and tips to get you back on your feet after job loss

iUniverse books may be ordered through booksellers or by contacting:

iUniverse
1663 Liberty Drive
Bloomington, IN 47403
www.iuniverse.com
1-800-Authors (1-800-288-4677)

ISBN: 978-1-4620-6424-3 (sc)
ISBN: 978-1-4620-6426-7 (hc)
ISBN: 978-1-4620-6425-0 (e)

Printed in the United States of America

iUniverse rev. date: 11/29/2011

To all those who have been downsized and/or experienced job loss.

Contents

PREFACE

I originally started writing my thoughts and experiences regarding my job loss in my personal journal, something I have done for years. As I was going through the process of job hunting and coming to terms with my new state, it came to me that there were many others out there who like me, had lost their jobs, but who unlike me, did not have the support and the teachings that I have had.

In writing this, I helped not only myself in being able to express my thoughts and feelings, but I hope to now help others by sharing my experiences and the lessons that I have learned. Sudden job loss can be difficult and stressful—not only to the individual, but to his or her family as well—and readers will benefit from this book by knowing that they are not alone in their experiences and from the useful job search advice I provide.

I would like to thank my husband for his unwavering support and my children, who kept me busy and grounded. I would especially like to thank Carla, my career transition consultant, who encouraged me to write this book when I mentioned the idea to her and who was so supportive of me during my transition. Thank you to all my friends who were there for me and to those who provided me with their stories and words of advice along the way. It is a changing world out there. Sometimes I think we are on a good path, other times I am not so sure. I do know that we are up to the challenges that we face and success is often just a matter of persevering and not giving up.

I have found a new job now, and I wish a happy ending for all those who are out there still searching. I have grown and learned from my experiences—and I know you will too.

1. DOWNSIZED

Downsized. Restructured. Re-engineered. Laid off. What words these are. These words are designed to make it seem less nasty, that it was just business. These words really mean you have been let go from the company, and you don't have a job anymore.

It happened to me. I didn't think it would. Oh, I knew the possibilities were there. I had survived numerous downsizings at my company before, both large, companywide significant ones and smaller, departmental ones. Always, it was someone else. I was valuable, or so I thought, so if they had to let someone go, it wouldn't be me.

I knew there were people—some who I personally knew—who were good people but happened to be in the wrong place at the wrong time and got caught up in the downsizings.

I remember a time when two perfectly fine employees transferred into the group next to mine. When the order came from up top that all groups were to trim by 10 percent, they were the first ones picked. Last in, first out. Gone.

Then there were the smaller downsizings. Not a large, company directed one, but departmental ones that needed to trim just by one or two employees in a few areas. Tim,[1] a wonderful gentleman with approximately thirty years of service, who had dedicated his entire career and life to the company, who was known for his depth of knowledge, who had worked long, hard hours when required and was well respected by his employees … he was let go. Someone who had been working for him told me that they just came in one day, said thank-you very much for your years of dedicated service, and walked him out the door. Gone.

---

1   Names have been changed to protect privacy.

Being immediately escorted out once you are informed you are being let go is common practice in many large companies. It is to prevent employees from taking proprietary information or items as they leave—and to minimize disruption in the office.

Tim was apparently angered by it after all the years he had put in. He was bitter that—despite all his hard work for the company and his accomplishments—they had dismissed him so abruptly. He felt that he was due better treatment. He felt that he was denied a happy, farewell retirement.

I felt it too. I was a lot further away from retirement—still several years before my fifty-fifth birthday. Being told that they no longer require your services is bitter. I was allowed some time to pack my personal belongings, hand over my laptop, Blackberry, keys, employee ID, security pass cards, and then I was escorted from the building—out of the building and the company that I had been with for twenty years. I had worked for the company for my entire career. I had applied during my final year at university and had been so happy to land the job. I had turned down an offer at another company just to be there. I had built my career around that company—and it had defined me. I walked out of the world that I had known for most of my adult life. What was next? I did not know. It was a void, an unknown.

Why am I writing this? For many years, I have written in a personal journal every few days to reflect on things, to help focus on my goals, to motivate myself, or to sort out my thoughts. Benjamin Franklin reflected on thirteen virtues every night to determine ways to improve himself.

This is a journal of my feelings and experiences—and a guide for the many of those out there who are going through, or will go through, what I have. It helped me to jot down my feelings and gives me a feeling of satisfaction that I might help someone else who suddenly loses his or her job but has not had the same support that I have had. Many people feel lost and cut adrift when forced to experience *downsizing*.

I was lucky. I worked for a large corporation that had a policy of providing the services of an external career transitions company for a period of time. Many companies employed this firm for varying lengths of time for their recently terminated personnel. The firm would have a consultant present who would come into the office immediately after the boss delivered the news, comfort the employee, give him or her a business card with their company's contact information, and let him or her know they would help them to find a new job.

It happened so fast. In my case, I had a meeting scheduled with my boss for eleven o'clock that morning to update him on a report I was developing—or so I was told. Around 10:30, he popped by my office cubicle and said gruffly, "I'm ready whenever you are. I have some time now."

"Sure!" I responded, and he left. I sent my drafts to the printer and quickly gathered up my materials. I picked up my printouts and brought them back to my desk to arrange and staple them. On the way back, I saw our HR director standing at the administrative assistant's desk. I had a good relationship with her; we had worked together in the past and had become work friends.

"Hi there," I called out. "Down for a meeting?"

"Uh, yes," she replied.

"I'd like to talk to you afterwards. Maybe we can get together for lunch?"

"Uh, maybe," she replied somewhat sheepishly, with a glance at the administrative assistant. I was oblivious, thinking she was worried about time constraints, and left it at that. I needed to get to my meeting. She must have known that I was being let go—and that I would not be there by lunchtime.

Not wanting to take too long, I gathered my things and walked briskly to my boss's office. I was buoyed in anticipation since I felt I had done a good job in designing the format of the report—even though the raw data was not firm and I was still in the process of obtaining more accurate, up-to-date values.

When I passed a senior manager in the corridor, I chirped, "Hi! How's it going?"

I had dealt with him on a regular basis and we had a good working relationship.

With a smile, he responded, "Great. Just great."

Little did I know that he was likely headed back to his office after having just let go one of his people who were located down the same hall as he was coming from. I learned later that several of his personnel had been let go that day. Many of those were liked by others, including myself. They were good people, and it still saddens me to know that they were affected as well—though in some way, it made me feel better that we were let go together. They were not bad employees and I hoped that I was thought of as one of the good ones too. Many felt their loss and spoke well of them and it helped to lessen the blow.

As for the manager, I knew him to be hard-edged, demanding, and goal oriented. He had completed his task. Now he would be able to make his numbers.

I hurried down the corridor to my fate. I went to my director's office and sat down, putting the reports on his desk. His stony look may have been due to tension or grimness. He said, "I'll get directly to the point. As you know, the business unit did not do well last year."

He kept glancing down at some sheets of paper in front of him. Were they notes on what to say, perhaps? At this point, I do not recall exactly what else he said. When it registered, I realized what was happening. He said it was a business decision, dozens of others were also being let go and I was not the only one.

"How many?" I had asked.

"Dozens," he had replied, declining to give me an exact number.

He told me that a consultant was waiting outside his office to talk to me. Tears welled up in my eyes. Sadness overcame me as I realized that my career there was over. He handed me a large envelope and told me to read the enclosed information.

I pulled myself together, and from a sense of responsibility, knowing that I was going to be gone forever and wouldn't be there to explain to him my report and what I had done, and from a sense of pride, to show him that I had done a good job, I said sadly "Well, shall I go over the reports then and I'll show you what I've done?"

"No. Take this time for you. This is about you now. Would you like to speak to the consultant now? She's very good and experienced and will help you." I could tell that he wanted to leave, escape and not have to face me any longer. He wanted to hand me over and be done with his responsibility.

I nodded silently, the tears beginning to flow as I tried to hold them back. He left hastily after introducing her and shut the door so we could talk.

She spoke warmly and kindly as she could see I was upset. I put on a brave face as she explained things. She gave me her card and a folder with information on their services. Having been with the company for so many years, I already knew what the next procedure was. I had to hand in all my company-issued items—cell phone/Blackberry, laptop, employee ID, security access cards, and keys. To protect proprietary company information and belongings, an administrative assistant often escorts the terminated employee from the building. It is usually a third party who had no involvement in the decision—likely so no anger is taken out on that person.

In some cases, once everything is turned over, employees are allowed to take their coat or purse before being escorted out. In some cases, you are allowed to go back to your desk and take your personal belongings. In other cases, they will pack your personal belongings and ship them to you. They offered to allow me to get my personal belongings during off hours— accompanied by the administrative assistant, of course. I went back to my desk, looked around, and decided to take my things. I didn't want to have to come back—plus I did not have much. I had changed cubicles recently and had purged many items. I knew exactly what I had and did not keep many personal items at the office.

My biggest challenges were some of my personal files that I kept on the computer. My personal phone directory and calendar were integrated with my work ones through the Blackberry. I had personal appointments and contacts listed. I needed to make copies.

There are many reactions to being let go: anger, grief, shock, and numbness. In this situation, professionalism is the best course. Anger and loud displays of emotion or physical acts gain you nothing—except to be talked about later as part of the office gossip. You want to leave with dignity.

I cried. I couldn't help it, but I held myself together and went bravely down the elevator. I thanked the administrative assistant for everything she had done over the years. She was blameless but had been put in an awkward position. She didn't know what to say other than to wish me well and to let me know that I could contact her if there was anything I had forgotten. No doubt, she had others to escort after me—many others were laid off that day. I might not have even been her first that day.

I later learned that two administrative assistants had been let go from our downtown office. The majority of our business unit had moved to a more suburban location two years earlier, about an hour from the downtown core. There were plans for consolidating the rest of the group there. Since the VP of operations and his directors were moving to the suburban location, they got rid of their administrative assistants and transferred their workload to the ones at the suburban office.

The remaining administrative assistants at the suburban office were quite stressed by the additional workload. The survivors of the downsizing were faced with double the work. There was nothing wrong with the administrative assistants who had been let go. They were just in the wrong place at the wrong time.

I went to my car, put everything in, wiped my eyes so that I could see clearly, and drove home.

Lessons Learned:

- Don't leave personal files on a company computer. If you are downsized suddenly, you might lose access to them and other information you may need—or leave behind personal or financial information that you might not want others to see.
- Go the way you want to be remembered. Maintain your professionalism. You don't need to thank your boss—after all, he or she just let you go—unless you felt that it was something beyond their control and you had a good relationship with him or her. However, you should maintain your dignity. Ask any

questions you may have and accept as well as you can what has happened. It does no good to get angry, upset, or loudly emotional. They will not change their minds.

- Be attuned to the warning signs. Remember that no one is immune. Yes, it could happen to you.

2. TELLING THE FAMILY

When I arrived home, I just sat on the living room sofa. I knew I had to call my husband and let him know, but I just sat there, numb, not really thinking or moving.

I dialed my husband's office and he answered immediately, likely knowing something was wrong. His phone display would have shown that I was calling from home when I should have been at the office. It may have been a problem with one of the kids, and I might have had to go home.

"What's wrong?" he asked.

"I was let go today."

"Oh." There was a long silence as he took the news in. "Are you okay? Do you want me to come home?"

"No. I'm okay." I felt a deep sadness and heaviness. *There, I had said it. I had been let go.*

"No, I can come home. Just give me a few minutes to wrap up some things, and I'll come home right away."

"No, there's no need. You can't do anything so you might as well stay at the office. I'm fine."

My husband knew that I was a pretty practical person. He always had a ton of things to do at the office and could not really leave. He was always working late or to the last minute. He was torn but knew that I was right. He couldn't change or do anything. He, too, was quite familiar with living in a world of ongoing downsizings and knew that I would have received a severance package, so we would be fine financially for the time-being. It would just be the emotional impact and having to deal with finding another job that I would have to go through.

"Are you sure? I can come home. Yes, I will come home."

"No, don't bother," I replied more firmly. I didn't want to have him home and have to deal with him as well. I had my own emotions to deal with. I wanted to be alone. I didn't want to have the burden of having him sitting here when I knew he had a lot of work to do. I was in shock and wanted to retreat into my shell. I just wanted to crawl into my hole and not face the world. I didn't want to talk about it, relive it, or experience the pain. I wanted to be alone with my numbness, my ending.

"Are you sure?" he asked with a touch of uncertainty. He sensed that I didn't want him to come home.

"Yes."

"Okay. You can call me if you need me. I'll come home early."

And that was that. It was over. He knew. I had been let go.

He did come home early. I appreciated the gesture.

When my twelve-year-old daughter came home from school, I said, "I was let go from work today. They had a downsizing and a number of people were let go, including me."

"You mean you're not working there anymore?"

"Yes."

"Does that mean you'll be home every day? Are you going to look for another job?"

"Yes, I'll find another one. We are okay for now. My company has given me a severance package, which means they have given me some money, so we are okay until I find another job."

"Oh. Okay."

I was calm and nonchalant and she took it in stride. Since I didn't look upset and it didn't look like something she needed to be upset about, she went about her ways as a twelve-year-old is wont to do.

That night, as my ten-year-old son was watching television alone in the living room, I sat down on the sofa near him. When there was a break in the programming, I said, "I was let go from work today."

He turned and looked at me with his eyes wide.

"You mean you were fired!"

I winced inwardly. I think he has watched too many episodes of "The Apprentice" with Donald Trump's trademark line: "You're fired!"

"No, it's not quite the same. My company was downsizing, which means they let go of a bunch of workers so they could save some money by having less people to pay. Don't worry. I will get another job somewhere else."

"Why don't you go work at Home Depot?" He liked going to the Home Depot near our home.

"No, I don't think so." I laughed. He was reassured that things were okay and went back to watching his TV show. I sat with him for a while before I returned to my household chores.

Lessons Learned:

- Tell it straight. For me, I felt it was best to not to beat around the bush, but to just tell my family simply. I got it over with quickly rather than thinking about it and spending time worrying over their reaction.
- Be calm when telling the children. It will only worry and upset them if they see that you are upset. If you act as if it is an occurrence that you will deal with, then they will be reassured.
- Children are resilient. I was surprised that the kids took it so easily and as well as they did. I suppose that my behavior made it seem as if there was nothing for them to worry about. I'm glad. There was nothing that they could do about it, so why worry them.

3. THE EARLY STAGES

Losing a job is like losing a family. You go through a similar grieving process. At the beginning there might be denial, anxiety, shock, anger, relief, fear, grief, shame, depression, or blame. You slide downhill in this early stage when your job has suddenly ended. For those who have been with the same company for a very long time, it is a significant loss.

For me, it was indeed a grieving process. I had been with my company for twenty years and had begun my career there straight out of university. It was a significant amount of my life spent there, with many memories and friendships formed over the years.

Even several months later, I sometimes felt that it was not real—that I was just on vacation and would go back to my office soon. I would have to tell myself then that, no, it's over. I couldn't go back. I was no longer employed there. I didn't belong anymore.

The psychological stages that you go through when you are downsized may be divided into three phases: ending, exploration, and new beginnings. These may be visualized by an upside-down bell graph.[1]

When you first lose your job and that part of your life has ended, you move down emotionally on the graph. Then you bottom out and go through an exploratory stage where you get reoriented. Stress, approach-avoidance, and general exploration of possibilities occur around here. Once you begin to have acceptance, you start to move upwards towards hope, energy, and enthusiasm for a new beginning. You start to see the new possibilities and directions that your life can take.

Some people fall into a depression after being terminated. If you experience symptoms of depression, such as prolonged feelings of emptiness, hopelessness, sadness, loss of appetite, changes in sleep patterns, then it may be beneficial to seek medical advice to help you through it.

I told myself—and was given pep talks by others—that perhaps the downsizing was a good thing and that I might end up with something better. It was a chance to have a new beginning, a chance to perhaps try something different.

My sister-in-law advised, "I always say a door closes on one thing, but many other doors can open up. This might be the best thing that could have happened to you."

"This could be like winning the lottery," said another friend, referring to my receiving a severance package. If I found a job at the same salary before the severance ran out, then I would come out ahead financially. *This could be profitable if I found a job soon,* I thought.

My friend had previously had an opportunity to take a financial package to leave his company, but he had chosen to stay. Many of those who had taken it were quite happy with their current situations. He always wondered if he should have taken it too. It was a risk. As his family's sole breadwinner, it was a risk he had dared not take.

It was one thing to hear and tell myself these positive things, but emotionally I was not at the new beginnings mind frame yet. It was one thing to hear and say that things will be better, but it was another to actually feel it.

Shortly after I was downsized, I ran into a neighbor. As we were chatting, I casually told him about my new situation. He was not someone that I knew well, having just moved into the neighborhood three years earlier. Since his home faced the other way, we did not see each other often.

I found it easy to tell him, without feeling upset, about what had happened. I found that it hurt more when I spoke to previous colleagues or close friends and I became emotional when they expressed their sympathy.

The neighbor told me how he had been laid off a long time ago. Shortly after, while he was jobless, he was diagnosed with cancer. His wife got into a car accident and their car was destroyed. His two sons were still young at the time.

He felt as if he had reached rock bottom and was in total despair that everything was going wrong in his life. He didn't know what he was going to do or what was going to happen. He eventually recovered, got a new job, and was doing very well and looking forward to retiring soon. He had triumphed through adversity.

Many people, when they learned of my situation, would tell me stories about how they—or their friends or family—had gone through similar difficulties and were now fine. All meant to provide encouragement.

While I was saddened by my situation, it did provide a measure of hope and optimism. I understood what they were trying to do, and I felt grateful. It helped me emotionally to learn about others who had been through what I had.

Even weeks later, it was difficult to speak with some of my former coworkers. With the abrupt downsizing, I had not had a chance to say good-bye to some of my colleagues and friends there.

They were very supportive, but I found that it brought back memories and the hurt that I no longer belonged there. Even when I thought I was over the emotional stage and could speak calmly about it with other people and had done so, when I spoke to past co-workers the pain would resurface. I preferred not to hear about what was going on back at my former place of employment. I wanted to forget and move on.

The analogy that losing a job is like a death of a family member is a good one. Time passes and you no longer mourn the loss as keenly. On a daily basis, I was fine and actively job searching, but then something would remind me of it. The memories and sadness would rise up—and my heart would be heavy again.

A professional who has dealt with many people who have been downsized tells anyone who is going through this experience to not go it alone. Don't wrap yourself away from the world and hide inside your cocoon. There is a natural tendency to want to withdraw when something like this has happened. Perhaps the shame, embarrassment, hurt, or despair makes you not want to speak about it. Find a mentor, a friend, or an outside networking group to talk with. Someone outside your immediate family can be subjective and provide you with the support that you need. Family members can be too close to you emotionally and are not as subjective in providing you the advice and support that you need. Don't cocoon. It might take you a while to come out of it. Some never do.

I did not hide the fact that I was downsized from my immediate family, friends, and acquaintances. It was a fact. I had made the decision, however, not to tell my mother.

My mother was in her seventies. My father had passed away from cancer many years earlier at the age of sixty-two. Due to her arthritis, she did not go out much and spent much of her time at home. If she had learned of my situation, she would have spent her days worrying. Since there was not much she could do about my situation, there was no point in burdening her with the knowledge. I told my sister, but I asked her not to let my mother know and she agreed it was best.

In most situations, I believe honesty is best. However, in the case of my mother, I felt it would cause her unnecessary stress. Every person's situation is unique. Whom you tell is a personal decision.

Lessons Learned:

- Losing a job is like experiencing the death of a family member. This analogy helped me to understand what I was going through, and that I was not being an emotional wimp.
- Endings, exploration, and new beginnings are the stages that you go through after you are downsized. It is normal to experience them.
- Things will get better. Once you begin to have acceptance, then you will begin to move emotionally toward hope, energy, and enthusiasm for a new beginning.
- People are supportive. Everyone was always encouraging—and many told me stories of others they knew who had gone through it as well.
- You are not alone. There are many others who have been downsized before.
- Some people fall into a depression after being terminated. Some of the symptoms of depression are prolonged feelings of emptiness, hopelessness, sadness, loss of appetite, or changes in sleep patterns. It might be beneficial to see a medical doctor for advice to help you through it
- Find someone you can talk to. Don't go it alone. Find a mentor, friend, or networking group to provide you the support you need. There is a tendency to cocoon and withdraw when you have been downsized—don't do it. Find someone you can talk to.

4. CAREER TRANSITION FIRMS

I was fortunate. I had the use of the services of an outside, independent career transition firm for a few months after my termination.

Career transition is an interesting term to use for the period when you are laid off and don't have a job. True, I suppose. I was in transition. Transition—transitioning to who knows where yet.

Career transition firms are also sometimes known as outplacement firms, a more descriptive but, to me, a harsher sounding term. You are now out as opposed to in transition.

There are many career transition firms. Some are very large with locations worldwide, and others consist of just one person who consults and works one-on-one. While my experience was only with a large firm, they were a valuable resource—much more than I initially thought prior to using their services.

A career transition firm helps you with job search skills. They don't find you a job. That can be done with employment agencies, recruitment firms (headhunters), and through your own efforts. They are more of a teaching and guidance resource to help you during your career transition. Of course, providing examples and help preparing a resume and cover letter are the first things that come to mind.

The firm I was with offered examples, tools, and resources to conduct a job search—and they provided me with information regarding various ways to go about obtaining employment. They provided information on the different types of recruitment firms, what to expect, which online sites might be beneficial, and what the best ways of finding a job are. Networking is the best. Newspaper ads are the worst. Samples of resumes, cover letters, thank-you letters, and tracking forms were some of the areas covered.

I found the webinars (like a live seminar, but conducted over the Internet so you can watch it on your computer in the comfort of your own home) particularly useful since you could ask questions of the instructor and interact with the other participants. Some webinars demonstrated using Internet sites to conduct an online job search or interview practice webinars where you could get feedback from others on your responses.

Much of the same information on job searching and interview techniques is available for free online or in books you can get from your local library or bookstore; however, it is nice to have all the information gathered in one place and to be given some guide for what to start doing.

A key benefit to using a career transition firm is the availability of a consultant with whom you can speak with and discuss your individual needs. They also provide advice, guidance, and support.

I had set up my first appointment to meet with my personal consultant early the following week. I was a few minutes early and waited nervously in the waiting room, dreading the possibility of running into someone I knew that had also been downsized.

I didn't want to talk to them. I didn't trust myself to not get emotional. I wanted to hold myself together and be professional for my first meeting. Maybe misery loves company, but I didn't at that point. Thankfully, I didn't see anyone else there that day that I knew. It was a large firm and had many clients from many different companies.

I was fortunate to be assigned to a wonderful consultant, Carla. She provided more than just professional job search advice—she provided emotional support. She was someone outside of friends and family that could provide impartial advice. Not only that, she was a wonderful person. We clicked early on and became good friends.

The consultants are not counselors. They are not trained as such. Their expertise is in how to go about finding a job. However, they have seen many people and many different circumstances and can advise as to what is best for you.

You decide how much you want to do on your own and how much guidance you want. Some people hardly meet with their consultant, choosing to just e-mail or call if they have a question. Others meet with their consultant on a weekly basis. Some just go through the webinars and Internet resources and leave it at that. You can choose what services suit you best.

If your company does not provide you with career transition services upon termination, you might want to consider going to a firm on your own. Fees will vary depending upon the career transition company, the amount of services they provide, and the length of time you engage them for. The three months that I spent with them was just right for me. Since it takes several months on average to find a job, having some support during that time is good.

Some will also provide ongoing support for free afterward. For example, the career transition firm I was with held networking sessions for an hour and a half every Friday morning. You could meet with others who were also in career transition to network and provide advice and support to each other. When my period with the firm was over, I was still entitled to attend the Friday networking sessions whenever I liked as an alumni of the transition program. I was also given access to the alumni website and its job search tools. This was a good resource.

Community organizations and other organizations also provide job search skills for free. My universities and professional organization offered career centres that I could access. I did not avail myself of their services since I was already with a career transition firm; however, they are there for those who need them.

Remember, whatever you do, don't withdraw and cocoon. Find a mentor or friend to talk to.

Lessons Learned:

- Career transition firms are a good resource. If your company doesn't provide you with their services, you might want to look into going to one on your own if you can afford it. It may be well worth it, especially if you feel you need help in learning job search skills.
- Community organizations, professional organizations, schools you have attended, or government-sponsored programs might also offer career centres and job search skill training that you can access at no cost.
- It usually takes several months to find a job. I found that having the services and resources of the career transitions firm for a period of three months was just the right amount of time for me. The right amount of time will vary depending upon the individual and their needs.
- Take advantage of everything a career transition firm has to offer. Read the material, take the courses, view the videos, attend the workshops and networking meetings, and meet with your consultant on a regular basis. It is up to you to make the most of it.
- Don't cocoon.

5. FINANCIALS

Once I was downsized, one of the first concerns other than finding another job was my financials. How long could I last without a paycheck?

I was fortunate to receive a severance package that would last me several months. I also had a spouse who was working so we still had an income stream, albeit halved. Still, I worried. I no longer had the security of a steady paycheck. Our family needed the two incomes. It would be up to me to make the most of what I had.

Most of what to do is common sense. Cut down on unnecessary expenses. Put off any major purchases you had been planning if you can. Keep to a budget. Consult with your financial advisor if you have one.

However, during this period I learned a few things that you might not be aware of, and I would like to pass them along in case you might not know of them.

Unemployment Insurance and Employment Insurance

In the United States, benefits are given to eligible workers who are unemployed through no fault of their own as determined under state law, and meet other eligibility requirements of state law[2]. These are known as Unemployment Insurance benefits (UI). UI payments are intended to provide temporary financial assistance to unemployed workers.

In Canada, this type of benefit also exists and is known as Employment Insurance (EI). Many years ago, it was also called Unemployment Insurance, but the Canadian government changed the name to the more logical sounding Employment Insurance. After all, there is life insurance to help with costs after you have lost your life, car insurance if you incur costs associated with your car, house insurance if something should happen to your house, and employment insurance if something should happen to your employment. However, it could be argued that it is insurance that is paid out when you are unemployed, hence unemployment insurance. I guess it depends on your point of reference.

Many other countries have similar benefits in the event of loss of employment.

In general, benefits are based on a percentage of an individual's earnings up to a maximum amount. The maximum is usually not a huge amount. Don't expect to be living extravagantly. At the time of this writing, benefits can be paid for a maximum of twenty-six weeks in most states in the US, and additional weeks of benefits may be available during times of high unemployment. You should check the rules for your location as this can change or can vary by region.[3] In Canada, you can receive EI up to a maximum of fifty weeks, depending on the unemployment rate in your region at the time of filing your claim and the amount of insurable hours you have accumulated in the previous fifty-two weeks or since your last claim, whichever is shorter.[4] As in the US, additional weeks of benefits may be available during times of high unemployment.

If you meet eligibility requirements in the United States or Canada, then you can access these funds. In Canada, if you have received a financial severance package, you are not eligible to receive any EI until your severance money has been used up.

What do you mean by used up? The government will calculate the equivalent amount of weeks that the severance pay represents. This is like having a salary for that period. If you are still unemployed after this time, you may apply for and receive the insurance benefits.

Even though you think you may find a job shortly—or that you have enough funds to tide you over for a while—you should file your claim as soon as possible. This is because it takes several weeks for them to process your application. If everything is already on file, then you will be able to receive your payments as soon as your severance runs out rather than waiting with no funds coming in until the application is processed. Also, very importantly, the amount of qualifying time you have worked is calculated from the date you file your claim.

Unfortunately, I didn't act on this advice right away. I had planned to find a job before my severance ran out. Optimism perhaps? Denial? I didn't want to be on government benefits—even though I had paid into the fund over my entire career.

Unemployed. I'd joined the ranks of the unemployed.

Personal Financial Management

Budgets or expense tracking are good ways to keep a handle on your expenses. A budget gives you a guideline or framework for how much you plan to spend and where. By tracking your expenses against this framework, you can determine where you are spending your money, whether it is in line with what you want, and whether you can cut back in an area.

Since I had been tracking my expenses for years, I already knew where most of our money went. If you haven't been doing this, draw one up to assess where you are financially.

You can also draw up a simple balance sheet and look at what you currently have in assets versus what you have in debts. From there, you can decide what your next steps might be. Various sample personal balance sheets and templates can be found easily on the Internet by searching under personal balance sheet.

Splitting Your Severance Payment

I consulted a personal financial advisor a few weeks after I was downsized. I decided to take advantage of this free service provided by my company to make sure I had all the bases covered. Since I had always kept a handle on my finances, I thought that I would already know most of his advice. However, severance payment was a new to me. I consulted with him in case he had some useful advice. If you have similar company benefits, take advantage of them. I was glad that I did since he provided me with a couple of suggestions that I hadn't considered.

One suggestion was that I could ask my company to pay me my severance payment over two years. For example, I could ask that I be paid half the money this year, and the other half the following year. It would be up to the company whether they would do this or not, but it might be an option that you could possibly negotiate. If you are only receiving a few months or less of severance pay, this is not worth doing.

The reason for splitting your payment over two years is to avoid a large amount being paid to you in the same taxation year. If you are being laid off toward the end of the year, then you would have already earned most of your annual salary. This large severance payment could significantly affect your tax bracket and the amount of taxes you would pay that year.

If, however, you were able to split your severance payment so that some of it was paid to you in the current year, and the remainder of it in the following year, then your tax burden might be lessened. This would be especially beneficial if you were still unemployed for a significant portion of the following year and in a lower tax bracket when your remaining severance payment comes in.

Since I had been terminated in the first half of the year, I decided to take it all in one lump sum. If I found a job before the following year, then if I had split my severance it would just add more to my full year income next year, so I might as well take it all in the current year of termination when I knew I would have some months with no salary coming in. Also, I would have more deductions in the current year since I would be able to shelter some of the severance payment in additional retirement savings plan contributions. It was better to do it in that taxation year in my particular case.

Examine your own situation to determine your best course of action.

Additional Retirement Savings Plan Contributions

You may be allowed to contribute part of an eligible termination allowance or retirement allowance directly into a retirement plan. This is something to check into because it will shelter some of the money from taxes that year. You can withdraw the money out of your plan in the future. The timing of your withdrawal can make a difference in how much tax you will pay for the year.

Mortgage Amortization Changes

Another suggestion you might consider is that you could lower your home mortgage payments—not by breaking out of your current mortgage agreement, but simply by changing the number of years you are amortizing monthly payments.

For example, suppose you currently have a five-year term mortgage with an amortization period (the total length of time it would take to pay the total mortgage loan) of ten years, and that you are three years into this five-year term. You still have two years to go before renewing your mortgage agreement again, possibly for another five-year term.

You could keep your original five-year term mortgage with the same interest rate, but by changing the amortization period to twenty-two years (the common length of twenty-five years used by many banks minus the three years you have already done), you could halve your monthly payments.

Of course, this means it would take you twenty-two more years to pay off your mortgage instead of seven. However, in the meantime, it lessens your current expenses. When you are employed again, you can change it back to what you had before.

There is usually a nominal fee for doing this; however, you can always discuss the possibly of waiving this with your bank manager given your lowered financial circumstances, which means you no longer have any money coming in to help meet the payments.

Being optimistic, I decided that I would hold off on changing my amortization. It would be unnecessary if I found a job quickly—and I wanted to pay off my mortgage sooner rather than later. If this dragged on and I needed the money, this would be a way to free up some monthly disposable cash.

Consulting with a Company-Provided Financial Advisor

Financial advice depends upon your personal circumstances, so it is best to consult an advisor to help sift through your options.

A benefit of some large companies was access to an outside firm that provided employee counseling and help. It was a confidential, free service that you could call if you had problems. No information was given back to the company except for statistical purposes. The services included drug and addiction help, counseling for depression, and dealing with stress.

Some of the less obvious—and likely not as accessed—information included finding elder care, daycare, nutritional guidance, financial advice, and counseling for your dependent family members. One colleague accessed it for counseling help for his depressed son who was in a car accident and had missed most of his school year. Financial advice was available for those employees who had personal debt problems or other types of financial questions. There were limits to the amount of time you could have; nonetheless, you had some access to an experienced professional financial advisor. It doesn't hurt to call; they could provide you with advice and information that you were not aware of. I called for advice on the best way to handle my severance package and got some good guidance.

If you are immediately terminated and no longer have access to this, perhaps your working spouse does. If so, you can seek financial help for your family through that route.

If you are not as fortunate, there are still many other places to go for financial advice—if you feel you need it. Check for reliable financial planners near you.

Lessons Learned:

- You should check the EI and severance rules for your location as this can change and can also vary by region.
- File your claim for UI or EI immediately after termination. It takes time to process and your qualifying weeks of employment are calculated from the date that you file your claim.
- Under Canadian EI rules, you are only eligible for employment insurance benefits after your severance payment runs out. This is fair. The EI benefits are for those who have no other funds.
- If it makes sense for your situation, see if you can have your severance payment given to you in separate payments over two years.
- You may be eligible to contribute additional money into your retirement savings plans where it will be tax sheltered.
- Track your expenses. This will make you more aware of where your money is going.
- Draw up a budget. This will give you a guideline on how much you are spending for what, and an indication of how long you can last without an income.
- Create a personal balance sheet if you do not already have one. Look at all your assets versus your debts. Various sample personal balance sheets and templates are available on the Internet.
- Seek advice for your personal situation. What is good advice for one person might not be good for another.
- Don't stress. Easier said than done. I worried about not having a salary; however, remember that this situation is temporary.
- Stay calm and take action. Taking positive action will give you some peace of mind that you are doing what you can and are moving forward.

6. EMPLOYMENT LAWYERS—DO YOU HAVE A CASE?

A few days after being downsized, I began wondering whether I was getting the right amount of severance. I investigated it.

Current Canadian employment law states that an employee is entitled to one week of severance pay for every year worked, up to a maximum of twenty-six weeks.[5] I had been given a reasonable severance package. I was grateful for this.

In the United States, there is no requirement for severance pay.[6] Severance pay is often granted to employees upon termination of employment and is usually based on length of employment; however, severance pay in the US is a matter of agreement between an employer and an employee. Ideally, you are with a company that provides a good severance package.

There are stories in the media about people that did not receive any severance and had to fight for it. I was fortunate and thankful that I had worked for a company that provided an amount to tide me over while I was in transition.

An old friend suggested that I should seek the advice of an employment lawyer to see if I could get more severance. When she had been terminated a couple of years earlier, after only working at her last place of employment for just a few years, she had sued and received fourteen months' salary.

I mulled this information. I had known that she had been terminated, but not that she had successfully sued for so much more.

I did not feel that I had any real case to sue for more money. I was being downsized, along with many others, by reason of business restructuring; I could not argue that it was a wrongful termination. I might spend a lot of time and money attempting to get more—and end up with less.

"They might give you more just to settle," she said. "They don't want the time and bother of a lawsuit, and the possibility of bad publicity."

In her case, she had been the only one terminated at the time and had other reasons—good ones—for wrongful dismissal. I decided in the end to let things be.

As if to support my decision, I spoke with another acquaintance a month later and learned that she had been terminated six months earlier and was suing for wrongful dismissal. At the time of our conversation, she had already spent $25,000 on lawyer's fees and the case was still not settled. She was stressed and didn't know if she should continue to pursue it. If she didn't, then all the money she had put in would be lost. If she did, then anything she received might all just go to paying the lawyer's legal fees.

In most instances, you can consult with an employment lawyer and get an assessment of whether they think you have a case or not. Some do not have an initial consultation fee.

Another acquaintance that had been downsized just a couple of years short of early retirement age decided to sue. She wanted to bridge the gap until she was entitled to receive a reduced pension. By being downsized before her retirement age, she had lost retirement medical benefits. She felt that she would have difficulty finding another job at her age. The initial consultation fee for her lawyer was $150.

She had decided not to join the class-action suit that was being prepared by others from her company. She pursued an independent case. The others felt that perhaps they were targeted because of their closeness to retirement. After all, it saved on future costs for the company, but there was no way of proving this. The company would argue that they were all let go in the name of downsizing, not age.

My friend did not join suit because they can drag on for years. A small case, such as hers, might be dealt with more quickly. Also, she believed she was not asking for a great deal and would be in a better position to negotiate and make decisions quickly for a settlement.

However, as a single case, the company might not agree in order to not set a precedent. They could afford to wait her out and let the case drag on. She decided to try anyway. It was worth it if she could get bridged to retirement. It sounded reasonable to me.

Her friend, a well-known lawyer, looked over her severance papers. He thought she might have a case, but he advised her to consult with a lawyer who specialized in employment law.

A couple of weeks later, she told me that the employment lawyer had advised her not to pursue it. He could, perhaps, get her an additional six months, but the costs, time, and aggravation involved would not make it worth it for her. Meanwhile, she would not have her severance money to live on while it went through the courts, since the company only gives the severance payment upon agreement with their severance terms. She decided not to pursue and signed her severance agreement.

She told me she was glad to have spent the $150 and gotten good advice and peace of mind from a good lawyer that specialized in employment law. I am glad she had an honest lawyer who advised her in her best interest, rather than charging her thousands of dollars pursuing it.

Lessons Learned:

- You may, by law, be entitled to severance pay. Check the severance pay rules for your location. is one week of salary for every year worked—up to a maximum of eight weeks. In my case, it meant that I was only entitled by law to only eight weeks' salary as severance payment. Thank goodness my company was more generous than that.
- Consult with a lawyer that specializes in employment law and has a good reputation. If my friend had not gone to a specialist, she may not have been given the best advice and might have pursued her case. The first lawyer she consulted was not an employment specialist and had thought that she might have a case. Someone who is familiar with all the labor laws and precedents is in a better position to know what you are entitled to and can likely get.
- Suing can be expensive. Make sure you have a case and that it is worth the expense and time involved.
- Consult with a lawyer that has a good reputation for integrity. Some lawyers may take on a case even though the odds of winning are low. Even if you win, you might not come out ahead by much—so decide whether it is worth it.

7. THE TOOLBOX

The basic tools for a job search are the resume and cover letter. They are the documents most needed when applying for a job.

I have compiled these tools at the end in a section I have called "The Toolbox."

There are many excellent books, references, and examples available on how to write a resume and cover letter. Check with your local library, bookstore, and the Internet. I recommend that you consult with these sources for ideas and information.

A good resource book that has been around for many years and is updated regularly is *What Colour is Your Parachute?* by Richard N. Bolles. The manual details how to go about conducting a job search and writing resumes and cover letters.

The Internet also abounds with examples. For example, Workopolis (www.workopolis.com) has a resource section with info on how to write a resume, ace an interview, negotiate an offer, etc.

In some fields, applicants are asked to bring a portfolio that shows examples of their work.

The following are some of the job search tools that I touch upon at the end of this book. My thoughts and comments can provide a foundation for you—especially to those who have not gone through this before, have not had to job search in a long time, or do not have the benefit of the advice and experience that I have had.

The following are the basic tools in the toolbox:

Tool 1: The Resume
Tool 2: The Cover Letter

Tool 3: Your References List
Tool 4: The Business Card
Tool 5: The Ninety Second Intro
Tool 6: Your Marketing Profile
Tool 7: Follow-Up Tools
Tool 8: Tracking Forms
Tool 9: Job Finding Sources

8. PUTTING OUT THE RESUME

The resume was the first item that I put together to see how it depicted my career, my accomplishments, and my life. This document can be a source of pride, bitterness, or despair. It is a history of where we have been and what we have done.

I had prepared a resume only a few times in my life and began my new one with some trepidation. However, it was not an onerous thing to put together after all. Formats usually follow a general standard. In that respect, I did not find it difficult.

I spent a great deal of time agonizing over what words to use—and how best to portray myself. In the end, I was happy with my final result.

After I sent out my first resume, I was extremely hopeful, thinking that my resume was strong and they would contact me. I received no response.

By the time I had sent a few, the fact that I was just one of many applicants had sunk in. I knew this intellectually, but the reality did not sink in until this experience.

In many cases, the only way to apply was electronically. Once sent, it disappeared into a black hole. There were no contact names to follow-up on its status, only variations on the ubiquitous: "We thank all applicants for their interest; however, only those under consideration will be contacted."

A friend had been quite discouraged by the black hole effect as well. He had resorted to researching the companies to try to discover who the hiring boss or department might be and actually getting to the person to speak with him. I was quite impressed with his resourcefulness.

I learned to tailor each resume and cover letter to accentuate my qualifications that were best suited for the particular job. I got nibbles here and there.

I once had a telephone screening interview, which gave me a contact name to follow up with. I was asked if I would be available the following week to come in for a live interview. I responded immediately that I was available, but when I didn't hear back regarding a date or time I followed up. The HR manager never returned my calls.

I assume that they had decided to interview someone else and couldn't be bothered to respond to me—one of the many applicants that they didn't have time to deal with. I felt that it was a reflection of the non-professionalism of the company. They could have easily let me know that they were considering other candidates. *I'm not sure this is the type of place I want to work for anyway,* I told myself. I was bitter about having to be subjected to this indignity.

I had another interview after which I decided the job was not for me. After I learned more about the details of the job, working environment, and conditions, I decided it did not suit my needs and the work culture was not a good fit. I sent an e-mail to the interviewer thanking him for his time and let them know that I would not be pursuing the opportunity. I was in the early stages of my search and I wanted to make the right choice regarding the job I would be doing for the next few years. I was not desperate enough to take anything that was offered.

I continued the search.

I did not search heavily, having decided to spend most of the time with my children over the summer. I decided to begin a serious job search in September, but I would keep my eyes open in case a good opportunity came along. I thought, *I was with my company for twenty years, I deserve a break.* Others told me this too. I hadn't asked for a break, but I had gotten one nonetheless. It can be difficult if someone is so upset during this time that the mind does not see this as a break. My time was quite filled up.

I wondered how I had managed to do everything when I was working. My husband pointed out that it was the same before we had kids. We were busy before, but once we had children, we marveled at how much free time we really had before they were born. It was just a different kind of busy. We will always manage. Our priorities and what we do just changes with our circumstances.

If I am honest with myself, my not applying to many jobs was also a way of avoiding all the rejections, from avoiding putting out resumes with no result. If I didn't apply much, then I could justify the poor response by my not trying very hard. Avoidance. I didn't care—I was taking a break. Avoidance. I was still not quite in the upward swing/moving forward emotional cycle.

Lessons Learned:

- Review the job search tools in the toolbox at the end for specific comments on each.
- Don't get discouraged. Keep on trying.
- Check out the work culture and whether it is a good fit for you. It may be a factor in deciding if you would be happy working there.
- Follow-up if you can. You can sometimes do some research on the Internet to find out who the hiring manager is and make contact.

9. NETWORKING

I had friends. I was friendly and got along with my co-workers. The majority of jobs are found through networking and very few are obtained through the newspaper. Networking would be the best means of obtaining a job.

I was bad at this. When I first contacted my friends, I got emotional. I was not ready.

I had a friend and previous co-worker who had been downsized well over a year earlier. After a long period of time, he had sent me an e-mail to keep in touch, say hi, and let me know that he was still looking. It was addressed only to me, though I believe he sent these to others as well. I had responded and wished him well. He sent me an e-mail every few months. After more than a year, he found a job.

After I was downsized, I contacted him. After all, he had gone through what I had from the same company. It had taken him about a year to get over things. He had been angry and depressed. He had worked his way up the company and didn't have the educational credentials for the work he was doing, but he was experienced and good at what he did. I knew this from having worked with him, but—on paper—it didn't look good that he didn't have a university degree.

He was supportive. He told me that networking was helpful, as well as using Internet tools to get background info. He even provided me with the name and number of an HR person at his company.

Another friend let me know that she had spoken to a mutual colleague of ours. When he had learned of my downsizing, he had told her that he had been downsized three times before. He said I could give him a call and he could give me some advice. I took him up on it.

When I called, he was very supportive and understanding. He told me that each time he had been downsized, either through company downsizing or dissolving, it impacted him emotionally. He told me that emotionally, the impact never gets easier. You are just able to bounce back and recover faster. The third time it happened, he contacted two hundred people within two days of being downsized, bouncing back quickly and tapping into his now established network. Each time he was downsized, he was able to find a new job within three months. I was impressed. I was not sure I even knew two hundred people to call. It was my first downsizing. I let myself wallow in my emotions.

Being independent, I hated to have to ask around and approach people. I preferred to find a job posting and apply on my own, but I knew that these methods were not as fruitful. I needed to learn to play the game right if I wanted to maximize my chances of winning. Unfortunately, I was busy wallowing.

After a downsizing, an old university friend had just about used up all his severance money when he finally landed his current job. He had used LinkedIn (www.linkedin.com) as a networking tool. LinkedIn is a very popular online networking tool and I highly recommend it. It is free and easy to use. It is similar to Facebook, which is an online social networking group; however, LinkedIn is used more for professional networking. Users create a profile and then contact and link with others whom you know to build your network. You can ask people in the network for information about a company that you might not get elsewhere, the inside scoop on what working conditions might be like, etc.

I attended a networking session at my career transitions firm. Sessions were held every Friday morning. I noticed that other networking sessions were listed in the business section of my local paper. They were open to anyone who wished to attend and were held in various locations. Sometimes there was a nominal cost, such as fifteen dollars.

At the networking session, there was a person who facilitated the discussion. We went around the table and everyone introduced themselves and gave a brief summary of who they were and what they were looking for. I was reminded of an Alcoholics Anonymous meeting. It was indeed a support group for those in transition. Members of the group provided encouragement and advice to each other.

Networking sessions are a valuable resource for those who do not have the benefit of a career transitions firm; they can help you with support and advice. It gives you others to talk to. They are all going through the same thing. They have been downsized.

A university classmate called to see if I was going to attend our twentieth reunion. I told him no, and let him know that I had been downsized. He offered to send me the link to the external job postings of his company. If there was any job that I liked, I could send my resume through him. Unfortunately, his company was an hour and a half drive from my home and I didn't really want the commute. *I might have to resort to this, though,* I thought. I checked the postings, but there wasn't anything that suited me at the time. *What did I want? I wanted what I already had before. I had lost it.*

Another friend let me know about a possible job opening. I got a lead from another who had heard of openings elsewhere. I sent my resume to both places. I got advice and job leads from these networks and I started to move forward.

Lessons Learned:

- Networking is the best method for finding a job.
- Try networking sites such as LinkedIn (www.linkedin.com) as a way to broaden your network base.
- Organized networking sessions for those in career transition can provide advice and support. Check for sessions in your local paper that might be available in your community.
- Put out the word. People are willing to help. If you let all your friends, family, and acquaintances know that you are looking for a job, they will let you know if they hear of any opportunities. They won't know if you don't tell them.
- Follow up regularly. Keep in touch with your contacts on a regular basis. People can easily get caught up in their own daily demands and may not be thinking of your situation after a while. It helps to remind them and to keep you fresh in their minds should an opportunity arise.

10. CREATING A PERSONAL BRAND

Personal branding is an interesting concept that is being used by more and more people. Creating your personal brand is essentially creating what you want your reputation to be. We are familiar with brand names of products. According to the Merriam-Webster online dictionary, a brand name is defined as:

> 1: An arbitrarily adopted name that is given by a manufacturer or merchant to an article or service to distinguish it as produced or sold by that manufacturer or merchant and that may be used and protected as a trademark
> 2: One having a well-known and usually highly regarded or marketable name

With personal branding, the idea is to distinguish you as a unique product, and to make you a well-known, highly regarded, marketable name. For a consultant, this is particularly relevant since they are marketing themselves and their expertise, but this concept can be applied to anyone who is out there looking to promote themselves and find a job. Even afterward, knowing and developing your personal brand can help in career advancement and for having a good marketable profile.

A personal brand is not just a name or trademark. It should convey what you are about, your personality, your image, your skills and attributes, what differentiates you from the competition, and why someone would want to deal with you.

When we think of a product brand, for example, a Mercedes, we tend to associate it with luxury and class. When we think of a Jeep, we associate it with a rugged, sporty look.

I tried to think of what I stood for. It is not as simple a task as for a product brand where the purpose is more defined. I am multi-faceted. I can do many things. I had to think on this a while. Defining your personal brand is an excellent exercise in evaluating yourself, what you have to offer, and what attributes you want portrayed and communicated. While developing my resume, I had to do some of this—but putting it in the context of a personal brand gave much more definition to who I am. My whole self. It is more than just what my skills are—it is my character and image. Who am I? This is who I am.

I had taken marketing courses that included branding, but applying branding concepts to myself was a different application. It took some thought.

Take a moment and think about your own attributes.

What is your personality like? The Nike brand is associated with high-energy determination, an athlete's drive, and focus. Its slogan—Just do it!—embodies this. What image do you want to convey? Are you outgoing? Analytical? A risk-taker? A thinker? Always willing to help others? Do you have a slogan or motto that sums you up?

Nike is associated with a high-quality sporty style. What is your style?

A personal brand should define your area of expertise. Nike has the expertise to produce sportswear specifically tailored to certain sports. What is your area of expertise? What are the strengths and skills that you have to offer? What type of jobs and companies do you fit with best?

What is your personal brand promise? Nike promises to deliver excellent quality sportswear. What do you promise to deliver? High quality expertise in an area? Creativity? People skills? The list is endless and specific to you.

What makes your personal brand different? What makes you a better choice? Compare this to what makes Nike a better choice than other brands.

How does your personal brand relate to your target audience? What key ideas do you want people to associate with you?

Having a strong personal brand instills confidence in what you have to offer—both from your own point of view since you have defined for yourself what you stand for, and for the employer or customer that understands your attributes. A strong personal brand can instill loyalty in what you have to offer, and perhaps can command a premium price. A good personal brand can reduce the employer's perception of risk and make the hiring decision easy.

Once you have defined your personal brand, the next step involves creating a personal brand plan on how to communicate and grow it.

You need to be consistent in how you portray your personal brand. A personal brand is something that you must manage. You want the best reputation possible. We are marketable products—though I prefer not to call myself a product. We can evolve our personal brand. Similar to a product plan, we need to look at how we want to grow our own personal brand over the years. A five-year plan can be developed to grow your personal brand and gain higher profile. What do I want to add in terms of skills and abilities? What do I want to change? How do I gain visibility for my personal brand? How do I want others to think of me?

Lessons Learned:

- Define your personal brand—your expertise, style, personality, image, skills, and attributes. What differentiates you from the competition—and why would someone want to hire you over someone else?
- Once you have defined your personal brand, create a personal brand plan. The plan should focus on how to effectively communicate your personal brand, how to publicly be your brand, and how to grow your personal brand.

11. SOCIAL MEDIA

Social media is an interesting term. It was not around when I was growing up, but now there are thousands of social media sites. Some popular social media sites are Facebook, LinkedIn, and Twitter. My children and their friends all have Facebook profiles. They post pictures, make comments, and keep in touch with friends.

LinkedIn is more of a professional network. Twitter allows the user to post short comments or tweets. Blogs are another form of social media where you can write or post things of interest, much like a diary, that others can view and comment on.

Social media are media which is used for social interaction. It is the use of web-based and mobile technologies to turn communication into interactive dialogue. Businesses also refer to social media as consumer-generated media (CGM). A common element amongst all definitions of social media is the blending of technology and social interaction.

If you haven't been using social media before, now is the time to start. Increasingly social media is being used to search out qualified people, keep in touch with people as they move from company to company, and to do checks on you. While there are lots of different social media sites, Facebook and LinkedIn are two of the most popular and give you a larger potential network. Some of the smaller sites may eventually die out as Facebook and LinkedIn grow even more in popularity.

A common misconception, particularly among time-pressed professionals, is that social media is mainly for social purposes. Since they are often very busy, they don't feel that they have time to be social and therefore don't bother using social media. It certainly was my perception. I don't have the time or the inclination to chat online and post pictures. In fact, what if I don't want others to know too much about me? Who knows who might be accessing my pictures? Even if I have privacy protection, only letting in people I know, who knows what they may innocently be sharing or allowing others to see without my knowledge. Assume that everything you put on your site may become possible public knowledge. Maintain your image and your personal brand.

I did not have a Facebook profile. At least, I didn't have one at the time. Not because I was not comfortable with the technology, but because I never felt I had time for it. I was busy enough with my personal life, family, and friends and didn't need additional social outlets. I was horrified when I went online and typed my name to see what might be present on the Internet and found a Facebook page of someone else with a similar name. What if someone from HR of a company I was applying to checked and mistook that person for me? What if that person posted pictures or comments that were not very professional?

I was amazed at the number of times my name came up—some for items that were actually about me and many about others with the same name. There were over a million references! References to items that I would never have thought of or knew would be posted on the web, such as a mention in a memory post done several years ago by the funeral home where the funeral of a relative was held. There was even a cookie contest winner announcement from a cookie contest I had entered with my son four years earlier. It was scary how much of my life was being documented. At least I could hide in some anonymity by having others with the same name so that one would have to sift through to find out what actually pertained to me.

It was certainly a good reason to create a proper Facebook page of my own that I could control the content of—a good reason for anyone.

When someone does do a search for you, the first items that are usually listed are sites that you own. Other references to you from other sites show up lower in priority. It is an excellent idea to create a social media profile such as LinkedIn or Facebook profiles so that you can control what is being seen and said about you by making sure your posts are up front. It becomes too much work for others to sort through the other links below to determine what items are about you.

More recent postings also appear higher in the listings. You can use this fact to your advantage to keep your profile front and centre. Also, if you have a negative posting by someone else, if you have several good ones afterward, the negative one will fall farther down the list and eventually may be so far down it is not noticed.

In the personal branding section, we discussed how to present yourself publicly and how to publicly be the brand that you have defined. Social media is a method you can utilize.

Social media can help you to build name recognition. Ideally you want to build name recognition with influencers. Influencers are those who can possibly influence others regarding you. They may be someone important or a subject matter expert. By being visible to them—by commenting on their work or adding valuable contributions—you can get noticed.

Blogs are regular postings that can attract quite a following. They can be like a diary of your thoughts, musings, or regular posts of advice. There are even blogs of just pictures that a person likes and posts for others to follow.

Book authors who want to create a following are encouraged to create and maintain a blog so that their fans can follow what they are doing. I currently receive blog postings from a business expert who muses about various items on a weekly basis. He sends a weekly e-mail with a link to his blog. After you read the blog entry, you may post a comment on it. From this, he gets feedback from the readers. We are reminded on a weekly basis about him. It is a way of reaching out to many people simultaneously.

You can keep track of your contacts with social media. For example, LinkedIn notifies users if any of their connections update their profile. Twitter operates as a real-time streaming of constant small bits of information or conversation. A user sends short comments (tweets) about what they are doing or thinking and followers can keep in touch. People can be updated of what is happening to you on a constant basis.

Some politicians have adopted using Twitter on the campaign trail to let people know what they are doing, their thoughts, who they are meeting, etc. Friends can use it to keep in touch with others on a daily basis. It is a very public forum, however, and it is difficult to know who is following your tweets. Screen names do not always convey who the real person is behind it.

Recruiters are increasingly utilizing social media, such as LinkedIn, to source people with specific skills that they need. It is possible to search for specific keywords that users have in their profiles. It is important to treat your profile similar to an online resume and to keep it current.

A salesperson I know was contacted by a company after their HR person found him through a LinkedIn search. They were looking for someone in sales with a particular expertise. They contacted him via LinkedIn and eventually hired him. Even if you are currently working, opportunities could result from your online presence.

Social media is here to stay—and we must adapt if we wish to survive.

Lessons Learned:

- Social media should be utilized to increase your professional network. It allows you to build and keep in touch with a large number of people—and recruiters are able to search online and find people they might want to hire.
- Be careful of what you post online. You must maintain your professional image.
- Remember to publicly maintain your personal brand—even if it is on a social site. You never know who may be looking at it—even though you have privacy control settings.
- Sites that you are own will usually come up first in an online search. By creating and maintaining your own social media sites, you have more control over what others see of you online. This is better than having other people post references to you that may not be what you want others to see.

12. INTERVIEWING

Interview questions can be broken down into various topics:

- What can you do questions
- What will you do questions
- How you behave questions
- How do you fit questions

Preparing for an interview felt like an assignment for school. You must prepare your answers, write them down, and rehearse. It helps to practice in front of friends or a mirror. I knew this, but I felt awkward doing it. It seemed contrived to rehearse answers. However, after I had tried rehearsing, I realized the wisdom of it. It definitely helps to be prepared and to know what you would like to say—rather than to come out of an interview wishing you had remembered to tell them a particular point instead of saying the first thing that popped into your mind. Rehearsing also helps you be smoother in your replies instead of fumbling for the right words when you are on the spot.

Interview Questions

Various resources available online or from job search books have extensive lists of various types of questions that might be asked. Most of them are fairly straightforward in an attempt to determine what skills and background you have that you can bring to the job and whether you would be a good fit with the company. I had to think for a while on some of them. Yes, it was best for me to be prepared. The following are some examples:

Can-Do Questions:

- Tell me about yourself. What qualifications do you have that you feel would make you successful here?
- What were your most significant accomplishments?

Will-Do Questions:

- In your last position, what were things you liked the most? The least?
- What are your long-range goals?

Behavioral Questions:

- Tell me about the toughest team or group you have had to work with. What made it tough? What did you do?
- Tell me about a supervisor who was difficult to work for. What made it tough? What did you do?

Best-Fit Questions:

- Describe your ideal work environment.
- How would a co-worker describe you?
- Why do you want to work for this company? Why should we hire you?

I had to think for awhile on some of them. Yes, it was best for me to be prepared.

Don't ask about vacation or other benefits. This is important and I bring it up because it is a mistake that many make. These can be discussed once you and the interviewer have decided that you are the best candidate for the job and you are in the negotiation stage. Otherwise, you will appear as if you are more interested in the benefits than in the job itself.

Appearance

I watched a video on interviewing. In a poorly done interview, the individual did not make eye contact—and he gave negative reasons for why he left his previous employer. Then they showed him sitting straight instead of slumping back in the chair, making eye contact, and appearing confident and dynamic. His reason for leaving was that he wanted to do more in the area and that would be more possible in the new company.

Positive body language is important. Looking positive and energetic makes a good impression. Eye contact is important and shows confidence. Go in with a smile, sit straight, and develop rapport with your interviewer.

Dress well. It doesn't matter if the interviewer is dressed poorly. You must make the good impression. If you come to an interview dressed poorly and not well-groomed, it says that you don't take the time and care to prepare well for things. If you are like this now, how will you be later when you have the job? It pays to invest in a nice outfit for interviews. You want to create a good impression. First impressions count.

I was anxious at my first interview—not having done an external interview for many years. Once it got going, I felt more relaxed. I answered and asked questions as we felt each other out.

In the end, I decided that it was not a job that I wanted. It was my first interview and I was not at the point of taking a job I did not really want. I was disappointed, but satisfied that I had made the right choice. Why go into a job where I might be miserable because it didn't suit me? I would be spending a good portion of my waking time there. I was not desperate. Maybe in the future I would be—but not then.

When I let the hiring manager know that I had decided that it was not a good fit for me and thanked him for his time, he was thankful that I had let him know early in the process. He wished me luck and told me he was confident I would find something else soon. I was not as confident as he was. I agonized over whether I had made the right decision. Maybe I should have taken the job while still pursuing other options. It would have been harder to find the time to look for a job I did want while working—and it would not have been fair to the employer who had just hired me.

Later, there was a major downsizing at that company. As the newest person there, I would have been more likely to have been one of the ones let go. I would have been at risk to go through another downsizing. Perhaps I was lucky to have decided not to pursue it.

I managed to get an interview with another company—and it went very well. I definitely liked the description of the position. I also liked the hiring manager that I would be reporting to. She told me that she had only one other candidate to interview before making her decision—and I was the best candidate so far. I waited with anticipation for word.

When it came, I was disappointed. There had been changes since the hiring manager first started the interviewing process. The incumbent had moved to another project in the company that was now put on hold, and was therefore available to come back. They would take him back and fill the position internally. She thanked me and told me she would keep me in mind if future opportunities came up.

I was not too hopeful that something would come up there in the near future. I sent a thank-you note to the hiring manager for letting me know. I felt depressed. My hopes dashed. My search continued.

Lessons Learned:

- Many interview questions are fairly standard. Check out books and websites for examples.
- Prepare your responses to typical questions. Many of the same questions will be asked by prospective employers. You don't want to blank out or give a poor example of what you have done. It also increased my comfort level to know what answers I was going to give to certain questions.
- Rehearse your responses. Practice in front of a mirror—with friends, family, or by yourself so that you don't stumble and hem and haw. When I prepared and rehearsed, it helped me deliver my responses more smoothly.
- Watch your body language. Sit up straight in an interview and look interested and engaged. Smile.
- Research what the company does and any current news on them, such as their products, customers, or competitors. If you are knowledgeable about the company and the position, it will appear to the prospective employer that you are interested in the company and not just applying to any job posting. Also, current news reports can tell you other bits of information such as their financial health, new products they are working on, etc. Do you want to work for a company that is going under financially?
- Don't ask about vacation and other benefits during your interview. These can be discussed once you and the interviewer have decided you are the best candidate for the job and you are in the offer negotiation stage. Otherwise, you will appear as if you are more interested in the benefits than in the job itself.

- Never run down your previous employer. This is just common sense. Badmouthing others always makes you look bad yourself.
- Always thank everyone involved in the process—even if you didn't get the job. Not only is it courteous and polite, you never know if another opportunity might arise there and you want them to keep you in mind.
- Keep your spirits up. There are always other opportunities. It sometimes takes several failures before you achieve success. The trick is to keep on trying. After all, it only takes one success to get a job.

13. NEWSPAPER ADS

We have had a newspaper subscription for years. I had rarely looked at the classified ads. I began checking them every day. Even if a job they are advertising is not suitable, perhaps the company is still worth looking into to see if they have other job postings that are more suitable. You can spend hours on the Internet looking at job postings.

I checked the jobs section of our community newspaper as well. I would have loved to find a good job near my home so that I wouldn't have a long commute. It would take me at least an hour—if not more—to get to a job in the city. At least two hours a day would be spent commuting. It would be extra cost and less time with my family. At the beginning, I could choose to be more selective about where I would work.

It's helpful to add yourself to an automatically generated e-mail career alert available on some company websites. If there are any new postings that meet your criteria, you are then automatically sent an e-mail listing. I added myself to some sites. This will save you time always rechecking those websites for new postings. Also, you can usually customize the search criteria so that they only alert you regarding postings that fit your criteria, such as geographic location or position type.

It was discouraging. The jobs were either very specific, asking for a particular type of individual with years of experience in a specific skill set, or they were low-paying, low-skill jobs.

I clipped out ads on companies I wanted to look into further. Statistically, newspaper ads are the least successful method of finding a job, but I didn't want to leave any stones unturned.

As I was driving one day, I heard a radio advertisement. The space agency was looking to hire two astronauts to send to the International Space Station.

I was quite intrigued. I was a voracious reader of science fiction as a child and had dreamed of going into space. Shortly after, there was a newspaper ad for it as well. A couple of months later, there was a posting for a justice of the peace, no prior experience required.

It just goes to show that interesting job postings can be found in the newspapers. I had been discouraged by the newspaper ads, but sometimes an interesting gem can be found.

Another unusual job ad that I came across in the newspaper was for mystery shoppers. Mystery shoppers are people who are paid to go to a store and pose as ordinary customers. They then fill out questionnaires on what they observed. Some companies do this to find information about their customer service. I had heard of mystery shoppers, but had never seen an ad for it. I had never been looking.

I mentioned it while speaking with a friend who was close to retirement. She was quite excited and told me she would love to do it when she retires. I might want to try it down the road, too. For now, I was looking for something steadier and better paying.

It was another interesting piece of information filed away...

Lessons Learned:

- Check the newspaper ads. You never know what might appear.
- Respond immediately. If it is in the paper, many others may have seen it and are applying as well. The position may not be open very long.
- Newspaper ads are one of the least successful methods of finding a job, but don't discount it completely. Some people find a job this way—plus it gives you an idea of which companies are hiring. The position posted might not be what you want, but you can look into the company further to see if there are any other positions available that might be more suitable for you.

14. TAKE HEART

I applied for many jobs and did not receive so much as a reply or rejection note. Many jobs requested that you e-mail or apply online. Once the resume and cover letter was sent, it was as if it disappeared into a black hole with the ubiquitous automatic announcement "Thank-you for applying with our company. We appreciate your interest and will contact you should we decide to pursue your application." In other words, don't call us, we'll call you. There usually was no follow-up name to contact.

Stories from friends gave me encouragement during these times. A friend told me of his downsized brother-in-law who had applied for many jobs and was not getting any interviews. All of a sudden, after seven months, he received so many interview requests that he had to use a whiteboard to keep track of them.

Another told me of her sister—a single mother with two children—who did nothing after she was downsized. She stayed at home and did not job hunt. My friend had been quite worried about her sister and what would become of her. After six months, her sister decided it was time, began a job search, and found a new job. She ended up quite happy at her new one.

An old classmate told me his own story of how it took months and he was almost out of his severance money before he finally landed a job. But find one, he did.

Not everyone has the luxury of taking time to find a job. Financial pressures can mount. However, take heart. Keep persevering. Sometimes one can be fortunate and will find something right away; other times, it can take longer and one must persevere. Luck is often a matter of preparation meeting opportunity. Keep searching and be prepared to grab those opportunities. Don't give up and despair. Take heart in the examples of others.

Lessons Learned:

- Finding a job could take time.
- Take heart. Keep persevering. That job could be just around the corner.

15. RECRUITERS

Recruiters, or headhunters as they are sometimes called, specialize in finding or recruiting employees for a firm. They basically match an employer's requirements with a potential employee. A firm will sometimes use a recruiter when trying to fill a position that they are having trouble finding a suitable person. Recruiters typically get 15–35 percent of your first year's salary, and are paid by the hiring company.

There are two types of recruiters:

- Retained: They have a relationship with the employer and have been retained by the employer to help them find employees.
- Contingency: They run strictly on commission

There are various categories of recruitment firms:

- Personnel or employment agencies tend to be contingency recruiters that get a commission for every position they fill. The salaries that they typically recruit for are minimum wage to $60,000. They deal with a wide variety of occupations or professions. Some specialize in temporary work.
- Recruitment firms typically recruit for salaries ranging from $40,000 to $100,000. The positions tend to be for sales representatives or professionals. They will interview you for an hour or longer to determine your skills, background, and suitability for positions that they currently have or may get. The positions tend to require specialized skills that the company has

trouble finding, and recruiters may approach qualified individuals who are working elsewhere to try to entice them.

- Executive search firms are usually retained recruiters who have been hired or retained to recruit for positions with salaries ranging $80,000 or more. They are looking for executives with specific skills to fill executive positions. These positions may not even be advertised in the marketplace.

Avoid recruiting companies that ask you to pay a fee for finding you a position. Fees are normally paid to the recruiter by the hiring company for finding you. If the recruiting company is charging you, then their source of revenue may be from the fees that you and other jobseekers pay them in the hopes of finding them a job—and not from dealing with hiring companies with actual positions available.

Check their website and have a list of questions to ask the recruiting firm, including what services they offer, what types of positions they deal in, how long they have been in the business, who are their client companies, and how they build their inventory of candidates.

Beware of requirements to stay in a job for a specified period of time. This limits your freedom should you decide you don't like the job. They may have had a hard time filling that position for a good reason.

Recruiters are notorious for sending out your resume without your permission. Some may try to solicit jobs by advertising a large database of people whom they have available to meet an employer's needs. However, it is important to present yourself in the best light to potential employers. You wouldn't want a generic resume floating around that doesn't highlight all of your specific skills for a particular job. Ask the recruiter if they check with their candidates before presenting them or sending their resume. You want to be in control of your information.

A way to keep your resume in control is to put a footnote at the bottom stating that the resume is private and confidential. Do not reproduce without the author's permission. Also ask the recruiter to check with you prior to sending out your resume to a potential employer.

When contacting a recruiter, be prepared with your resume and an introductory statement positioning yourself and what you are looking for. Be prepared to discuss your skills, strengths, and accomplishments. Know your salary requirements—and what you no longer want or are unwilling to do even though you may have done it in the past. Be prepared for a hard sell to convince you about a job you don't like—just so that they can fill the position and earn their commission. Good recruiters will not do this; however, be prepared because some will.

How many recruiting agencies should one sign up with? Is it better to sign up with as many reputable ones as you can to maximize your chances? Or is it better to just stay with one company? The most common recommendation from several job search experts I asked is to sign up with just one or two—three at a maximum. If you are with a good firm, you can establish a relationship and they will work in your interest as well as the hiring company's. Also, a recruiter may be less inclined to work with you if they know that you are with someone else—and they may be quick to go with someone else.

If you are interviewing for a job that you have found on your own, don't tell your recruiter. They may also approach the company and present several other candidates that they represent and you will have more competition.

Less than 10 percent of people find a job using recruiters—so, while this is a possible avenue to employment, it is not the best one. As mentioned before, networking is the best way to find a job.

Lessons Learned:

- Investigate potential recruiters. Make sure that they are reputable and have a list of questions prepared to ask them.
- Sign up with only one or two recruiters. Don't spread yourself around with everyone, hoping to maximize your chances. A recruiter will be less inclined to work with you if they know that you may go with someone else at the drop of a hat.
- Less than 10 percent of jobs are found through recruiters. While this is something you should look into, don't rely on it heavily.
- Avoid signing up with recruiters who ask you to pay a fee for their services. Typically recruiters are paid by the hiring company. If they need you to pay them, do they really have many job placements?
- If you are interviewing for a job that you have found on your own, don't tell your recruiter. They may also approach the company and present several other candidates that they represent and you will have more competition.
- To avoid or reduce having your resume sent everywhere without you knowing, place a footnote at the bottom of your resume stating *Private and Confidential. Do not reproduce without the author's permission.*

16. JOB BOARDS

In the past, job boards were large bulletin boards where job notices were posted. These boards are still around in some recruiting or employment centres, though they are not a very efficient means of finding out about a job.

In today's world, job boards are Internet sites where jobs are posted. There are many where you can search for jobs or post your resume so that employers can find you. You can narrow your search for jobs by using keywords or selections, including location, type of area, company name. This makes it a quick and efficient method of searching for job postings that meet your requirements. An example of one is www.workopolis.com

Beware, however. While there are many legitimate job postings, often there may be postings which a recruiter is using to try to get more people for their roster of available employees. Recruiters get a commission from a company if they can place you in a job there so they want to have as many available people who might fit the company's requirements in their database. Even if they don't have a current requirement, they might like to have your resume on hand in case something comes along that they can use you to fill. Job boards have become a popular place for recruiters to search.

"What's wrong with that?" you might ask. "If a recruiter can find me a job, that's okay. In fact, that would be great."

The recruiter may send in your resume to a company and you might not have had the opportunity to tailor it so that it highlights your skills that best suit that particular job. It may have been a job that you might have applied to on your own, but now a company discounts you because they have seen your resume already and decided that you are not the best candidate.

Recruiters often don't have time to promote you to potential employers.

They are merely filling orders. Your resume could end up being propagated to many places that you are unaware of. A few people told me that they had been applying to positions posted on job boards, but the only responses they ever got were from recruiters. The recruiters were just collecting resumes to populate their inventory. They found it difficult to find a real job that way.

However, statistics show that people do get placed. It is a very inexpensive and efficient way to post a job listing so that thousands of people can see it—and for job seekers to search and find available positions. If you are aware of the potential pitfalls, it could be a good source.

Lessons Learned:

- Internet job boards are another source of job listings.
- Be careful about posting your resume where it may be public for all to see. You don't know who will get it or what they will do with it.
- Recruiters often search through online job boards to find new candidates.

17. NETWORKING GROUPS

I am a bit of an introvert. Personality tests say that I am between an introvert and an extrovert—I have attributes of both.

A ski instructor once told me that he was an introvert who had learned how to be an extrovert. *What an interesting way of putting it,* I thought. I think I fall into this category myself. By nature, I love nothing better than to be by myself with peace and solitude. However, I get along quite well with others and am considered sociable. I doubt others would consider me an introvert except my husband. I think I have learned to behave as an extrovert around others, but I am really an introvert who loves to be alone.

Of course, this introverted tendency may be because I am so busy. I am always dealing with multiple demands and tasks, but I crave the quiet moments to myself. A report by the Canadian Institute of Wellbeing indicates that women are more time-crunched and stressed than ever.[7] I believe it. I see it among my female friends. We want nothing more than time alone. Unfortunately, I had some additional time—but not under circumstances of my choosing. There was no real rest and relaxation because of the pressure to find a job.

I had been poor at creating a large network of friends and acquaintances. One of my old friends from high school, now a busy surgeon, confided once that because of his limited personal time, he had to pick and choose whom he wanted to spend it with. He had lots of friends, but had made a conscious decision of who to keep in touch with. Some others fell by the wayside, but I was one of his keepers.

I had not kept up with many friends, but my decision had not necessarily been conscious. It felt awkward to call someone after having been downsized. When you are downsized, you should reach out to everyone you know and let them know you are looking for a job—even if you haven't spoken with them a long time. I was embarrassed —it felt as if I was only calling them because I needed them, as if I was using them.

Of course you could always put a positive spin on it. "Hi. I haven't talked to you in such a long time, but I'm downsized and I have the time now. I would like to reconnect."

The majority of jobs are found through networking. You can join numerous networking groups. Some are free or funded by government or community groups, but others are mini-businesses that provide guest speakers, courses, resume services, and an opportunity to network with others.

For an introvert, joining networking groups is even more important as it helps broaden an introvert's social network that they might not otherwise have.

I was reluctant to join one at first. I was told of the benefits, but I was reluctant to be with all the others who were downsized. Would it be like an AA group? "Hi. My name is … I was downsized." I procrastinated.

I heard from another downsized person that she had joined one and that it was really beneficial. I decided to try it out. She was right—it was quite beneficial. If anything, it was like a support group. We were all there because we had been downsized. Everyone was very supportive. It provided motivation to hear about what others were doing and trying and to hear tips on what to do. Yes, I did have to stand up at the very first meeting and introduce myself. However, since I had been downsized, I got used to telling people about myself, my skills, and what I was looking for. This was a good venue to practice.

Lessons Learned:

- Most jobs are found via networking.
- Networking groups are very beneficial. There are various ones that you can join and I highly recommend it.
- Large, professional networking groups are good. There are membership fees; however, they can be worth it for the guest speakers and services that they provide.
- Introverts can learn to behave as extroverts.

18. ENTREPRENEURSHIP

*B*e *your own boss. You'll never be rich working for somebody else. No risk, no reward. The bigger the risk, the bigger the reward. Many great ideas and businesses started in the basement. Get out of the rat race. Own your own business.* All the commonly heard slogans exhorted me to consider the possibility of owning a small business rather than going to work again for another company. It was an interesting concept, but not one that immediately appealed to my risk-adverse self.

Startup capital would be needed. The odds of a small business succeeding are very low. In fact, they are terrible. According to the website of SCORE, a non-profit association dedicated to educating entrepreneurs, two-thirds of small businesses in America survive for at least two years, and 44 percent survive at least four.[8] In other words, the majority fail. The hours for many small business owners are long and hard, though many will say it is worth it when it is all work directly for your own self and profits.

Large businesses today first started off as small companies. I was intrigued by the thought. It represented a chance to strike out on my own—but doing what? What type of business? I did not know. There was no hobby or interest that I had that I could turn into a successful business. There was so much competition out there.

The career transitions firm I was with offered courses in entrepreneurship. The course would help you to assess whether starting your own business was a route you wanted to pursue, and then go over all the steps required. It was a multi-session course divided into parts, including drawing up a business plan, assessing financial requirements, and sources of financing. I had the time. I wasn't working. I thought that I might as well take it. So I did.

Many government and local organizations offer courses and/or counseling

57

on starting your own business. They can advise and help you to get started—and point you towards sources of financing.

I took the first entrepreneurship course offered by my career transitions company, called Entrepreneurship Part 1: Exploring. It was for people like me who were exploring the entrepreneurship possibility. The number one mistake that is made by those starting out is not doing enough research before embarking. This is common sense, but many fail to heed this advice. People can be blinded by what they think is a great idea, but they don't realize all the possible factors that could impact their business greatly.

We were warned that the hours were usually long and not to expect a large salary or to be earning as much as we had before.

There are many plus sides to owning your own business, though. There is pride of ownership. You can't be fired. After all, you are the boss. You don't have to retire at sixty-five, but you don't have company benefits either—unless you purchase them for yourself.

I have a relative who has her own small business. While she takes great pride in it, it is also a source of stress, and she spends a lot of time managing it.

For some people, it represents a dream. It represents a chance to be independent—a chance to grow their business into something large and successful. The profits are all yours. But so are the losses.

It almost seems like a lottery to me. A few entrepreneurs can make it big, but the rest are not worth much or nothing at all—risky tickets to freedom.

It could be argued that these calculated risks can be mitigated by doing your research, having the right product, and marketing it successfully. Research is paramount. Make sure to do plenty of research to increase your odds of success.

I didn't have anything in mind that I believed I could start a successful business in. I didn't have the guts to try at that point in time. The failure rates were not encouraging to me. I didn't want to be on my own. I had a family to support. I didn't want to risk our family money on a venture I was not sure would succeed. I decided that it was not for me. I decided not to take the remaining entrepreneurship courses. You need to be passionate and believe in what you are doing in order to make it succeed. I didn't have that passion.

Lessons Learned:

- Research, research, research. The number one mistake is not doing enough research before starting a small business.
- Two-thirds of small businesses survive at least two years. Only 44 percent survive at least four.

- Don't expect a large salary or to be earning as much as you did before.
- If you have a unique skill or expertise, consulting might be a viable option.
- Get advice and help. There are many government and local organizations that will advise you on starting your own small business. You might also be eligible for small business grants or loans.

19. CONSULTING

A few of my friends have gone into consulting. A few have done it successfully for years. If you have good, marketable skills, then you can sell your expertise. This is like having a small business—however *you* are the product. Your overhead is typically a lot lower since you can quite often set up your office in your own home or work on the client's site. If you have a home office, you can write off expenses on this portion of your home, lowering your income taxes.

Consultants can usually charge much more per hour for their services. They are selling their expertise at a premium, especially since it is short term. Several successful consultants I know have done very well financially for themselves. They love the freedom to pick and choose what they want to do and when they want to do it.

One was faced with the option of gaining full-time employment with the client—at a lower amount than what he was making as a consultant of course—or just having his contract end normally. He chose to continue as an independent consultant. When the contract ended, he went to another contract with another company. He enjoyed being his own boss and making lots of money.

I know a mother who sets up her contracts so that she can work from her cottage during the summer or times her contracts so that she can be away with the kids.

On the negative side, one friend who forayed into the world of consulting for a year found it stressful going from contract to contract. There was always the uncertainty of not being able to land another contract. Also, she found the marketing and unsuccessful job pitches demoralizing. She did not like spending time preparing a proposal—only to be rejected. She went back to working for companies after that. Consulting is not for everyone.

Another type of consulting involves almost a freelance, collaborative effort. A graphic artist I know had been downsized from a large firm. She decided to form her own graphic arts company, composed of herself, and set out to look for work. While she did do work on her own for clients, when there was a need by a firm to do a large job, then she, along with a few other independent graphic artists, were called together to work on it as a team. They knew each other and would call upon each other when there was work and help needed.

A friend in the film industry also depended upon work calls like these. When a crew was needed, people would contact him, and he would be employed for a period of time. Depending upon your profession, this might be a workable option for you.

On the downside, it can sometimes be stressful not knowing if and when you will get another contract once the current one is done. You must constantly market your services. You do not have company benefits. You may spend a great deal of time meeting with people and putting proposals together without being hired. It is important to be able to deal with rejection and to not let it affect your self-esteem.

While I had good marketable skills, I did not think I had a unique expertise that would make me a consultant who was in demand. I moved on to other options.

Lessons Learned:

- If you have a unique skill or expertise, consulting might be a viable option.
- Consultants can typically charge more per hour than they would earn as a salaried employee since they are providing short-term expertise. Their overhead is usually low since they can often work from home offices or at the client's site. They must get their own benefits.
- It can be stressful trying to obtain contracts and not knowing what will be available once the current one ends.
- Research. As with starting a small business, which a consulting business essentially is with your expertise as the product, good research is important to success.

20. FRANCHISING

There was a single morning course offered on franchising. Having taken the entrepreneurship course and deciding that it was not for me, I did not think that this would be a viable option. However, I wanted to keep an open mind.

I was also intrigued by the concept since a friend of mine had applied for a franchise with The Second Cup, a coffee shop franchise, and had been turned down. I was interested in learning more about how franchising worked. Since I had the time and it was only for a few hours in the morning, I decided to go to the session.

I found that there was much more to franchising than I had expected. I found that I was largely ignorant about it. I had associated franchising with stores such as Tim Horton's, McDonalds, The Second Cup, Molly Maid, and fast food chains. I thought franchises were fairly similar among them all. I was about to learn more.

What exactly is a franchise? According to the Oxford Dictionary, a franchise is a license granted by a government or company to a person or group allowing them to use or sell certain products.

A person pays an initial franchise fee and ongoing royalties that give them the right to distribute the products; however, the control of the product and brand image is usually done by the head office. This gives uniformity to the product so that customers generally know what to expect—no matter which franchise location they go to.

You need to apply to a franchise company and they will decide if you are the right candidate.

The seminar presenter was a very nice gentleman, looking every bit the professional businessman. He was from a franchise consulting firm, called

FranNet. I had never heard of a franchise consulting firm before, but I had not been exposed much to franchising. The consultant took us through the world of franchise ownership.

Most people don't work for themselves because success is not guaranteed so there is risk. Businesses cost money to start—and running a business takes talent and skill. It is basically because of fear of failure that people don't work for themselves. I could relate to it all. It was why I had decided not to pursue starting my own business.

We can, however, manage and reduce fear by doing our research and making fact-based decisions.

Franchising is different from having your own small business since you are part of a large chain with greater marketing and support. The concept has been tried already and has been proven successful. In many instances, you get support and training since it is in the interest of the entire franchise chain for you to do well and best represent their product and brand name.

You can contact other franchisees and talk to them about their experiences and ask for advice before you purchase. If you are from a different city or area, you are not a competitive threat to them and they can give you an honest scoop.

There are different types of franchise structures. There are ones that operate business-to-business and only during normal business hours. There are ones that are retail concept that have no site or inventory. There are ones that you can manage part-time and still work at a regular full-time job, which is something that I had not known or thought about before. The part-time ones are also appealing to those who want to still do something when they are retired. I liked that concept.

Half of franchises are under a full investment of $125,000. Cheaper than a house—and it can earn you money and eventually pay for itself.

Only 10 percent of franchise owners are in the same type of business as when they were employed, so you didn't need to have industry experience to be successful.

They claim that studies have found that franchise new business startups rarely fail—and when they do, it is typically because the franchisee did not stick to the franchiser's systems. The franchise has a proven business model and you have the benefit of their experience.

What I found even more interesting was the nature of the franchise consulting firm. According to their brochure, FranNet is the world's largest network of franchise consultants. They provide a broad array of services that include help in learning about franchising, researching your business, indentifying the right structure and strategic mix of the business, and introducing you to the franchisers that fit your model. Instead of going from place to place, you can get all this information at once.

What is even better is that there is no cost to you. They operate similar to a real estate agent. They help discern your particular buying criteria—and help you select one that meets your needs. From their knowledge of what is available, they can bring a few prospects to you. They are paid if—and only if—you find a franchise that you buy, and it is the franchisor that pays them, not you. They are paid a portion of the fees you would pay to the franchisor—whether you went to the franchisor directly or were introduced to them by the consultant.

In other words, the franchisor pays the consultant for finding suitable candidates for them. The franchisors work through the consultants because they help find the best potential franchisees, people who have a high chance of success. The prospective franchisee gets good advice and help from the consultant because it is in the consultant's best interest to create a happy match so that they will get repeat business and good referrals for their services. It seemed similar to how a real estate agent worked, but the consultant never made that comparison. He compared it to how an executive recruitment model works.

I was definitely much more interested in the franchising concept, but was not yet ready to do something like that. If I eventually did, it would certainly help to have a franchise consultant to help me navigate through the process of deciding what to buy and how to research it properly.

I liked the part-time franchise concept. Something to do while retired. It was something to build equity in and leave to the kids one day.

I was glad that I went to the session. I learned something that might be helpful one day. You never know where the future may take you.

Lessons Learned:

- There are many, many different types of franchises in many different types of industries. Franchises you might not have even thought of or considered—or not even realized that they were franchises.
- Franchise consultants are available—at no cost to you—to aid you in selecting a franchise company that best meet your goals.
- Many franchises are cheaper than buying a house—approximately half of franchises are under a full investment of $125,000.

- Franchises have a better chance of succeeding than starting your own small business. They have proven business models, but you should still conduct your own research thoroughly.
- Research, research, research. Research helps you to manage your risk.

21. CHANGING CAREERS

Being downsized can be an opportunity to change careers. Perhaps you have always wanted to do something different—or perhaps you just want to try something new now that you have a chance. It is something that crosses the minds of many once they have been downsized. I asked myself the same question.

At the local unemployment centre, there were several free courses and workshops for the unemployed to help them determine if they wanted to make a career change. I enrolled in one of them—a three-day career explorations course.

One of the first things they had me do prior to attending the course was to fill out a questionnaire. The questionnaire was designed to help match my responses to similar response profiles of people in various career fields. The idea was that if our responses were similar in terms of our interests and personality traits, then perhaps those careers would be a good match for me. This is a good exercise if you aren't sure what career or field you might be best suited for.

The assessment was called the Strong-Campbell Inventory, which matched my answers to an inventory of answers given by people who worked in various industries.

After the results were obtained, I met with a counselor to go over the results. High on the list of the career matches for me was the military. *Hmmm, I don't think so.* It is not what I wanted to be doing, but I do prefer structured environments. Luckily the other matches were more along what I would have predicted.

The counselor explained that the matches indicated that my responses were similar to those who were in the military, but did not mean that this was a career that I should necessarily go into. There were also indicators of how strong the correlations were so you could see if it was a strong match or not. One of the matches was with the career that I was already in, so at least it meant that I was suited to do what I had been doing already.

The next step was to attend the course itself. On the first day, we completed some other personality tests. We discussed how knowing and understanding what type of personality you were—and what type others were—helped you to deal with one another better. Also, certain personality types are suited better for certain types of jobs. Self-awareness is important in determining what you might be suited for.

On the second day, we were shown how to use a software tool to explore various career choices. It was a software program that we could access online that contained a huge database of various jobs with job descriptions, necessary education, average salary, and the demand forecast for the next ten years. This program was also used in some schools to help students research potential careers. I was quite fascinated at the opportunity to check out the data on various interesting jobs.

The other students were also looking at career changes. They were currently unemployed, which was one of the conditions of being able to take the course.

One participant was a tradesman who felt that he was in a declining trade. It was difficult to find work so he wanted to get into something else—perhaps in the green energy area installing solar panels. Another had been a supervisor in a manufacturing plant. He had been downsized and wanted to get into the health care field, which he felt was a growing and more secure field. He was thinking of becoming a medical technologist. A couple of ladies had both been in the financial industry and were looking to move into fields that were growing and more stable. Most of us were middle aged. Only one was young, in his early twenties, and his desire was to move out of the automotive sector to a better career.

We were guided through how to look for various pieces of information and then given time to research our individual topics. The time flew by as we explored the different realms of possibilities. What was even better was that we were given online access to the database and could access it from home—even after the course was done.

It was an excellent exercise. The grass always looks greener elsewhere and making a career change means potentially starting all over again. It is important to get as much information as you can about another career before taking that step. Maybe what you are doing suits you the best anyway, and you just need a change of pace somewhere else. You can at least leverage your experience instead of starting at the beginning.

Don't be afraid to change careers, though, and get out of an industry that may be declining. It may be a very wise move. If there are no longer many jobs in your area of expertise, it is probably better to go into a growth industry where the jobs are more plentiful and growing. For example, the health industry is predicted to expand greatly as the large baby boomer population ages and requires more health care services.

Essentially, before making a career change, you should ask yourself the basic questions: what, how, when, where, and—most importantly—why?

Why is the most important question because it is a significant step for a person to start a new career. You must understand why you want to do it—and why that particular career. Without a really strong reason, there is no point in doing it because in the end it could be a waste of time and money.

Some people pick a different career because it pays well or appears glamorous. The benefits of these could soon wear off if you don't actually like doing it. The best job is one that you are passionate about and suits your personality and skills—so that your job is enjoyable and you don't mind going to work every day. After all, if you must spend most of your waking hours doing it, it is important to get the best fit possible.

I had the opportunity partway through my career to hear a CEO of a major company speak to a group of students. He told us that the reason he believed he had done so well in his career was because he really enjoyed doing what he was doing. He would wake up most days eager to get to work and do more things. He worked long hours, but it didn't feel like work. The promotions came naturally as he began to excel at what he did. He said that the best career was a job that didn't feel like work. He admitted that there were tough times he sometimes had when there were a lot of problems to deal with and it wasn't so enjoyable, but the good times far outweighed the bad and that there were probably no careers that didn't have some rough spots that also made you appreciate the good times. He was fortunate to have a job that suited him so well, and he recommended that everyone spend the time to find a job that they liked and then put their energy into that.

He made a lot of sense to me. I had heard things like this recommended before by teachers and counselors, but to hear someone who was actually living the experience was inspiring. It is one thing to be told and another to learn that it could truly be done. Many years later, I met a university professor who basically said the same thing—he loved being a professor and didn't consider it work. I would like to aspire to a dream job that I couldn't wait to get up and go to every day. In my experience, this seemed to be a rare occurrence for many people, but at least one can try.

In addition to why, you must also determine the how of getting into a new career. Do you have the skills already? Do you need to go back to school for retraining? Does it cost you to get into it?

What is also a very important question to ask. You may think you know what a job entails, but the reality might be different. A good way to determine this might be to speak to people who are in the field you are considering—or go on a site visit.

A student in my career explorations course shared the story of how he had thought he would really like to become a medical lab technician. He called up a medical lab and told them he was thinking of making a career change, and asked if it was possible to meet with someone to ask a few questions for a few minutes. He did not know the person beforehand. This type of meeting is known as an information interview—you interview with a person or company representatives solely for the purpose of getting information and not for a job.

The person that he met with was extremely helpful and ended up giving him a short tour of the lab. When he showed them the lunch room, another employee opened the fridge to take out his lunch. Also in the fridge were stored test bottles from the lab. At that point, the prospective student said his stomach churned and he realized that he could not, in fact, work with lab samples after all, and that it was not the job for him.

Talking to people in the industry can give you advice and perspectives on it that you might not find otherwise—and it is worth the time.

The when is the question of how to best time it. Can you do it right away? Will it take time to get things ready or put in place first? If you need to go back to school, when do the courses start and how long will they take to finish?

The question where can be an important question involving lifestyle consideration. Where are the jobs located for this career? Will you have to move in order to pursue it? Are there many job opportunities in this field?

Thoroughly determining the answers to these questions will help determine if changing careers is right for you.

Lessons Learned:

- Career counseling may be available at your local unemployment centre, community centre, or school career centres. Take advantage of these services if you are considering changing careers. Many of these are free and are provided as a community benefit to the unemployed.
- Career interest or personality assessments are a good way to see if you might be suited to a particular career. There are various tests

available to help understand your personality style and interests and how similar your personality might be to other people who choose a particular profession. This is good to know and might point you toward a career you might not have considered before, but might be suitable for you. These tests are not perfect, however, so always keep that in mind when deciding.

- Career databases. There are databases available with descriptions of various careers, their typical activities, necessary education, and the salary range. They are very helpful when you are trying to research information about various careers. They are often available at unemployment centres, schools, or other places that provide career counseling.

- When considering a career change, determine the answers to the why, how, what, when, and where of your change before doing so. It is important to have all this information before you start—rather than finding out later that it doesn't suit what you want.

- Information interviews are a good way of finding out more about a job. Speaking with people who are actually doing the type of work you would like to do—and visiting places where they employ people in those type of jobs—can provide you with a lot of information and more of a feel of whether it would suit you.

- Find a job you love. If you enjoy your work, it won't feel like work. This is an ideal job to be in. This is when you have the opportunity to upsize to something better than you had before.

22. GOING BACK TO SCHOOL

For a career change, it is often necessary to go back to school to get the required skills. Or, you may just need to upgrade skills you already have or add to your skills to make you more marketable. Perhaps you want to get a diploma or degree that you always wanted—but never got.

A thought that often goes through the minds of those who have been downsized is whether to go back to school. It passed my mind and I considered it. Maybe I should get into another career and do something else. Maybe I should get out of sectors with constant downsizings and into another profession that is not as fluid.

I decided that I couldn't afford to and needed to find a job, but the thought lodged, and would pop up again occasionally. I would like to get another academic degree. I would like a change. I would like to drop out of the rat race for a number of years. It would be nice to live in my own world of study and seclusion and not struggle with the turbulence of the outer economic world and the demands of the paymaster. I would like to learn new things and enjoy the thrill of mastering a subject in an environment of encouragement and stimulation.

I didn't mind the thought of going back to school—studying, writing, and taking tests. But could I afford it? More importantly, did it make sense?

It was a difficult decision. In cases where you lack many marketable skills, going back to school is certainly a good decision. You need to have marketable skills in order to land a job. In cases such as mine, looking at a career change may or may not be economically better or more satisfying. Sometimes the grass looks greener on the other side, but—in reality—it has negative weeds of its own.

If it is a career that would make you happier, it may be worth the time and effort. However, it would also mean starting over from the beginning as you reestablish yourself—not to mention the financial cost of the courses and the loss of potential income while you are at school. One of the reasons that I decided to take the career explorations course was that I had had the time to take it and it was worthwhile to spend a few days exploring these options.

Answering the questions of why, what, where, how, and when are also applicable for exploring this option and should be done with careful research. The potential impacts to your family while you spend time pursuing this must also be considered.

As an adult considering going back to school for skills upgrading, there may be government funding or community programs to help you with this. It is worth taking the time to find out if there is such help available—and whether you qualify for them—so that you don't have to pay for the courses yourself. Check out local unemployment centres, government agencies, and schools.

Many private schools offer various types of training. Make sure that you check out their credentials carefully and ask about the successful job placement rate of their graduates. There have been scandals in which some private colleges were charging large fees, but offering substandard training that didn't allow their graduates to easily find jobs. Make sure that the school has a good reputation—or you may be wasting your time and money.

Another option can be learning on-the-job. Apprenticeships—where you work under someone who oversees and trains you—fall under this category. Electricians, plumbers, and many skilled trades offer apprenticeships.

You may feel that you don't have the prerequisites to get into the courses that you want. Many institutions have programs for mature students to help them upgrade their skills quickly so that they qualify for entrance—or they may evaluate your skills or past courses to see if you can be given equivalency credits. Call the school to find out. There are other avenues to explore, depending upon your circumstances.

Since going back to school involves a lot of time and effort, you want to make sure it is the right choice.

Lessons Learned:

- If you are considering going back to school, answer why, what, where, how, and when before doing so. During the course of finding the answers, it can also help to determine if this is a suitable option for you.

- Check to see if there are government or community programs available to help you with funding. You won't know about them unless you take the time to find out.
- Investigate the schools. Check the schools you are thinking of attending to see their credentials, whether their programs and training are well thought of in the workforce, and how successful their graduates are at finding employment. You don't want to waste your time taking courses—only to find out that it didn't provide you with what you needed to get a job. Some private schools are just scams—be careful where you go.
- If you don't have the required prerequisites for a course, call the school to see if you qualify for any waivers or if there are any suggestions for how to best meet the prerequisites.

23. ECONOMY NOSEDIVES

The front page headline in the local paper declared that we were now "on the road to recession."[9]

Fear gripped me again. It had been a few months since I had been downsized. Recession means more terminations, less jobs. I feared that I might not find one.

There were jobs out there—other lower paying jobs that I could land. You always read about people taking jobs below their potential to make ends meet. On the other hand, you may also worry that they might look at your resume and think you are overqualified and you will leave as soon as you can land a better job (likely true) so they won't bother spending their time on you. They want someone who will stay after they take the time to train you in their particular job requirements.

I decided to stay the course—and not let fear overtake me.

Another article said, "Historic observatory sold."[10] It was an article about the David Dunlop Observatory, the site of the largest telescope in Canada. They were no longer able to conduct world-class astronomical research there due to light pollution from encroaching urban sprawl. One particular paragraph caught my attention:

> I received a phone call ... telling me that operations of the observatory were ceasing and that my services were no longer required," said DeBond, who has worked at the seventy-three-year-old observatory in Richmond Hill for over seven years ... When the news came this week, that didn't lessen the blow.

A phone call… Your services are no longer required…

Heide DeBond had been anxiously waiting the announcement for a month, but it might be even harder having to wait. Maybe it was a relief to know it was over and to be able to get on with it.

In the business section, "Airline workers face turbulent skies!"[11]

Jazz jettison 270, American sheds up to 6800 as rising oil and jet-fuel prices eat away at profits. The deep cuts followed similar moves by the North American airlines. These include:

    4,000 at Delta Air Lines
    3,000 at Continental Airlines
    2,550 at United Airlines
    1,700 at US Airways

The headlines kept shouting. Companies were downsizing everywhere. There was talk of recession and a global economic slowdown.

Things were not isolated to where I was living. It was happening everywhere. The downward spiral continued.

> Parts maker in retreat … No turnaround seen after Vaughan-based Progressive Moulded eliminated 2000 jobs North American auto woes roll on … Merrill report says GM bankruptcy possible if the US auto market continues to tumble … Stocks sink as growth fears mount.[12]

A couple of months later, in just in one day, the following news items[13] showed that the malady was widespread throughout the world—a cancer creeping through and affecting lives.

Germany:

9,000 jobs cut in bank takeover … German insurer Allianz is selling the bank. It is a deal that will trigger one of the biggest rounds of job cuts in banking since the markets crisis began.

Britain:

Britain on brink of recession … Pound falls against euro, dollar latest sign nation's worst economic crisis in sixty years looms.

France:

Renault. Cuts hit 4000 workers ... Renault SA, France's second-largest car maker will cut 4,000 jobs in the country.

Italy:

Alitalia. Labor seeks sale input...newspaper have reported that 5,000 to 7,000 jobs could be lost from a workforce of 20,000.

China:

Olympics lower China's metal demands ... The overall junior market has simply melted down in the last six to twelve months.

Japan:

Land of the falling stocks ... the Nikkei is off more than 16 percent since the start of the year.

All of the above bad news was in a section that only consisted of four pages. This was not a good time to be laid off. There were a lot of people out of work, competing for the jobs that were left, in a time when companies were reluctant to hire.

24. STRESS

I had a friend and her family over for dinner. She told me that she was going to enjoy the food because the next day she had to go on a strict diet. Apparently her immune system was weak and she had suffered a lot of illnesses that year. Her iron levels were very low.

"Is it due to stress from work?" I asked. I knew that work had been very busy with lots of additional hours on her part.

"Yes, it could be due in part to stress. Every time I think it is going to tone down, something else comes up."

I was sure that it was. We wear our bodies down trying to keep up with the demands being placed upon us.

Just after I was downsized, I contacted an old friend and mentor to tell her my fate. In a coincidence, she had been let go that week too. We met for dinner.

We had met when I first joined the company. When she was forty-five, our company offered financial packages to entice employees to leave. It was one of many downsizing plans throughout the years. Her pension would be vested and she would get a nice chunk of money to go. She took it, wanting to do something different. She was tired of the corporate life. After a year at consulting, and several years at another company, she landed her dream job. It paid well, and the hours were good.

Then a new boss came in that summer. Just as she was about to go on vacation, she was let go. She had not even met the new boss, though she had been trying to schedule a meeting with him. She was replaced by someone at much lower salary than she had been making. She sued for wrongful dismissal and got additional severance pay.

She was unemployed for a long time before she took a job at a small company doing work similar to what she had been doing when she first started her career. The job was below her capabilities, but she needed to help support her family. She had a son entering high school and her husband's salary was not enough for them. These days, two income families are generally needed. My family needed two.

She had been sick more that year than she had ever been in her life. She had been struggling with coming in to work while being ill and had been off a lot (a factor that I am sure contributed to her being let go). I am sure it was the stress of doing a job she didn't feel suited for and worrying about her financials. Her health was bad, and she was depressed. I was depressed after meeting with her.

If you dwell on all the negatives, you get more down. It sounds hokey, but you must concentrate on the positives and have gratitude for what you have. Otherwise, the stress will build and accumulate and your immune system will wear down.

Exercise and eating well help combat stress. I lost weight during the first few months. Some people gain. Neither extreme is good for you.

Exercise causes the chemical release of endorphins in your body and gives you a happier feeling. It is sometimes called runner's high. Exercise builds up your stamina and actually gives you more energy to make it through the day.

Your body and immune system needs to be well-nourished to combat the effects of stress so it is important to eat healthily.

It's not easy to say, "Look on the bright side," when you have financial worries and your self-esteem has taken a beating, as in my friend's case.

However, things can always be worse. What good are you to yourself and others if you are sick? What purpose does it serve?

I couldn't help it. It was just happening to me. I know that there have been many times when I thought of something and the sadness welled up, but you must move on. Recognize that you are grieving, give yourself a bit of time, and then move on. Focus on the positive.

I had a lot of sleepless nights initially. Even though I was tired and would fall asleep right away, I tended to wake up in the middle of the night or early in the morning and not fall back to sleep. Thinking thoughts ... reliving events ... pondering the future and options. Lack of sleep puts additional stress on your body.

It was frustrating to tell myself that I needed to go back to sleep, that I had only slept a few hours, and I would be tired the next day—but I found myself thinking about one thing or another and was not able to. Finally, morning would arrive and I would be tired instead of refreshed. I didn't like the idea of taking sleeping pills and perhaps becoming dependent upon them, so I didn't take any.

I found that getting up and doing something for a while used up some of the restless energy and I was able to go back to sleep. Otherwise, I would lie there trying to go back to sleep until it was time to get up—at least I got something done. I wrote this passage at three o'clock in the morning.

This might not work for you, but it did for me. I would wake up, do something for an hour or two, and then even if I didn't feel sleepy, would then be able to fall asleep if I went back to bed.

These things will pass. Like sleepless nights that are spent awake with a newborn, you might wonder when it will end. Can I keep on doing this? However, that stage passes and things get better.

Try yoga or meditation. These techniques can also help to relieve stress. The deep breathing exercises in both are beneficial in helping you to feel calmer. I have found that deep breathing seems to be a common element in many stress relieving techniques.

I learned, too, to keep a positive mental attitude and to not stress myself over the fact that I couldn't sleep sometimes, which would just add more stress. It is often our own mind and thoughts that can sometimes be our enemy. How we approach what is happening can make the difference.

I am reminded of stories of survivors of horrific conditions. These survivors were able to think positively and hang on to life despite terrible conditions and the likelihood of death. They had a purpose for living.

A nurse once told me that, in her experience, the patients who came in with a good positive attitude and character, usually recovered faster for the same medical condition than those who came in bemoaning their state.

Give thanks. Take a journal and write down each day several things that you are grateful for. Focus on the positives. It will help you mentally.

Many books talk about mental attitudes. *A New Earth* by Eckhart Tolle[14] is a bestseller and I found it had many interesting concepts—and it helped me during this time.

Tolle talks about how the greater part of human pain is unnecessary and much is self-created. The pain that you create is always some form of no acceptance. The accumulated pain is a negative energy that occupies your body and mind, hence his term, the emotional pain-body.

A key thought for me is that we can stress over what has happened and review it over and over, however the past is the past and we cannot change it. We can think and dwell on the future and stress about what may happen, but the future hasn't happened yet and we can't do anything about it since it is part of the future. The present and what we are doing in this very moment are the only things that we can currently experience and control. So if you are feeling pain right now, step back mentally. Acknowledge how you are feeling without passing judgment about it. Recognize it—and by recognizing and acknowledging the pain, you may feel the intensity lessened. The pain-body is diminished.

We experience what is happening to us in the present. Whatever we may be feeling—extreme joy or extreme pain—after time, both will become memories and less intense. So we must live in the present since that is all that we are experiencing right now and can control. Don't let the present pass by and be caught up in dwelling on past or future events that we can't control.

Take a walk in a natural surrounding and live in the moment. As Eckhart Tolle said, the present and what we are doing in this very moment is the only thing that we can currently experience and control.

My career transitions consultant helped immensely with my emotional stress. I didn't want to create additional stress on my husband. It helped to talk to someone else about what was going on.

It sometimes helps to talk to your friends and family, rather than keeping it all in. I know that the words of encouragement, plus the stories that I heard, of others in similar situations pulling through, helped me feel better.

Another book which I found very inspiring and helpful during this time was *The Last Lecture* by Randy Pausch.[15] It is a true story by a man who was diagnosed with terminal cancer and only had a few months to live. He was a professor and he gave a last lecture to his students. His lecture was not about dying, but about living and the importance of overcoming obstacles, of enabling the dreams of others, of seizing every moment because "time is all you have ... and you may find one day that you have less than you think."

I had lost my job—not my life. Randy Pausch died while I was writing this. I am thankful for having had the opportunity to learn some of his wisdom. He told his stories and his advice in such a wonderful way. It is a small book and a quick read. I highly recommend it to everyone.

He also says, "We cannot change the cards we are dealt, just how we play the hand."

I had been dealt a bad hand, but I was still in the game—the game of life. I still had the opportunity to keep playing, to keep living. The next card could be a turning point. Thank you, Randy, for helping remind us to keep things in perspective—and for imparting your wisdom on life.

Lessons Learned:

- Keep a positive mental attitude. Stress is often self-imposed. How we choose to deal with it makes the difference.

- Exercise. Exercise causes the chemical release of endorphins in your body and gives you a happier feeling. It is sometimes called runner's high. I have never felt high when I run, but I do feel good that I am exercising and getting fit. Exercise builds up your stamina and actually gives you more energy to make it through the day.
- Eat healthily. Your body and immune system needs to be well-nourished to combat the effects of stress.
- Get enough sleep. In the early days after I was downsized, I did not sleep well. When you can, give yourself adequate time to rest and rejuvenate. Lack of sleep puts additional stress on your body.
- Give thanks. Take a journal and write down each day several things that you are grateful for. Focus on the positives. It will help you mentally.
- Talk. It sometimes helps to talk to your friends and family, rather than keeping it all in. I know that the words of encouragement, plus the stories that I heard, of others in similar situations pulling through, helped me feel better.
- Channel your energy towards doing something constructive. Don't wallow in your misery. Get out there and do something.
- Read inspiring books or self-help books. These can help focus you in the right direction.
- Try yoga or meditation. These techniques can also help to relieve stress. The deep breathing exercises in both are beneficial in helping you to feel calmer. I have found that deep breathing seems to be a common element in many stress relieving techniques.
- Take a walk in a natural surrounding and live in the moment. As Eckhart Tolle said, the present and what we are doing in this very moment is the only thing that we can currently experience and control.

25. THE DOWNSIZINGS CONTINUE

I like to run in the morning. I run for about a half-hour every other day. I run while my husband and children are asleep. I enjoy the early morning when everything is still and the birds are chirping, and you only see the occasional dog-walker. After my children were born, I had stopped running—no time or energy—and only in the last couple of years had started running again. Early morning was the only time that I could find that seemed to work out. Once I got caught up in the demands of the day, I could never find the time. In the evening, I was too busy with the kids, going places, attending to never-ending household duties, or too tired. The morning was when I could go out and have some quiet time to think, and to feel good about having gotten some exercise.

They say that exercise is a great stress reliever. I often felt emotional after I was downsized. On some mornings, I would just run as hard as I could. It was good that it was in the early morning and there were few people about. There were two times when the tears came streaming down, but there was no one to see. When I wiped them, they blended in with the sweat.

After a few months, I relished my run, looking at the flowers and trees, and the peace of the rhythm of my running pace. I still thought about things, and was sad sometimes, but often I was fine and enjoyed having the time to think and reflect.

On the radio, I heard that a large telecommunications company had announced that they would be letting 2,500 management employees go. That was equivalent to 6 percent of the entire employee base. They did not mention what the percentage was of the management base, which would likely make it a much higher percentage, since there are fewer managers than unionized staff. It's easier to get rid of management. There is no protection there. It is the same in other companies with union and management. It was just another major downsizing.

The father of my daughter's classmate worked there—and he was not one of the survivors. I believe the mother was a stay-at-home mom. Another family affected. The downsizing was all around me.

Downsizing has become a common business practice. Gone are the days of my parents' generation when many worked for the same company their whole career. Even when I started my career, downsizing was already occurring among companies. I had survived numerous previous downsizings within my company. In some cases, it is the right thing to do—otherwise the company might not survive. In other cases, I am not so sure. It might be a benefit financially in the short-term; however, they are getting rid of expertise and working personnel that might impact the company in other ways. In all cases, the victims are the people who are the ones downsized.

I called another friend who worked in one of the large companies that was downsizing. I hoped that her boss would not be affected by the downsizings. It looked like he would be okay. They had already downsized two others on their team, and there were only four to begin with. They couldn't afford to go down anymore. He would assume more responsibility. I was glad he was safe. He had two boys and a wife who worked part-time. A year later, they had another downsizing that he did not escape.

Another person, promoted the previous year, was taking possession of a new house the following week. Now he was downsized.

Another friend said a matter-of-factly, that he was sure that there would be lots of other horror stories. I was surprised at his hardened reaction. Perhaps he was just steeling himself against it. People expect it now and the casualties are just part of the expected outcome.

Morale at my friend's company was very low, a commonplace occurrence both before and after a downsizing. Often the survivors of a downsizing are traumatized as well. They have seen their comrades go—and they must shoulder the work left behind. They have been spared, but at a cost, with the knowledge that next time it could happen to them.

26. AGE

A few months after I was downsized, I had lunch downtown with a couple of friends. There was downsizing going on at their company. One of them was not too concerned. She was pregnant and had just had her maternity papers signed. She was safe and would come back when the cuts were over. Of course, our talk gravitated to the downsizing. It was on everyone's mind.

My other friend mentioned that an employee in his group was very nervous about being cut and would probably have difficulty finding another job since he was an older man—fifty-one. "Did you say fifty-nine?" I asked, thinking I had heard wrong. "Fifty-one," he replied. My friends were in their mid-thirties.

I was quiet. He had forgotten that I am older than I look. I was past mid-forties—not too far from his definition of old. Would the years of employment in my resume scream to others that I was old? I hadn't really thought of that before. I had thought it represented years of experience, but maybe it was a hindrance—at least I was below fifty.

Not long after, I was watching television. Something I rarely do. There was a commercial by the Colorectal society. In the ad, a boss was introducing a youthful new hire to an older fellow. The boss said that the new person would be doing accounts payable. They left and the older man said, "I do accounts payable." The ad faded to a black screen: At fifty, watch your butt. Then the screen faded to a display of the ad sponsor, the Colorectal society.

It was meant as some black humor with double meaning. That at fifty years of age you may start to develop colon problems so you need to watch your butt, but also at fifty years you need to watch out for younger workers being brought in to replace you. This is a commentary on our corporate society, that age is looked upon negatively and older employees are let go of in favor of younger ones. It is also quite telling about how widespread this perception was that it can be used in an ad where it was believed that most people will understand the implied meaning.

When I was coordinating a get-together with a couple of friends, I proposed a date. One declined and proposed one a month later. It occurred to me then that cuts were happening where she worked and that perhaps she thought she would be one of them and did not want to meet with us just yet. She was in her lower fifties and likely at the high end of her salary band. She was a prime target for downsizing. They could keep someone younger and cheaper to do the same job.

My friend was single and supported herself. She had a large mortgage and the circumstances saddened me.

That week I went to my weekly Dragon boat practice. I was on an all women's team which practices once per week together. A teammate had been worried that she would be downsized. Her boss had been cut the previous week—and she felt that she was at risk. She was fifty-one. I asked her if she was still there.

"No," she replied. "This is what they do to me after thirty-three years of service."

She was also single with a mortgage. She planned to consult with a labor lawyer to see if she could get a better package.

Lessons Learned:

- In my opinion, age is a factor. Though by law, companies cannot discriminate and let you go because of your age—when it comes to a large company downsizing, it is an easy way for companies to let you go as part of the general terminations. You cannot prove that age was a factor in their decision. However, an older employee is usually at a higher salary and the company can keep a younger, lower-paid one to do the same job. It might even be that the boss doesn't mind older employees and likes you, but is being more compassionate for the younger employees, figuring that the younger employees have a large mortgage and young family to support and you are close to retirement and more financially secure. In any case, beware—even if you have been doing a good job.
- Keep your skills up. If you are valuable and have good experience, this can influence their decision. If you are downsized, you are more employable elsewhere.

- Take advantage of company training budgets. Many companies have courses—or will reimburse you for courses. Do not put it off because you are too busy—a common excuse. Your future could depend upon it and it will not cost you to take them.
- You can take your training with you. My mother used to say, "They can take away all your possessions, but they can't take away your knowledge."
- Never indicate your age on your resume—though they will likely get a sense from when you graduated school and your employment history.

27. IT'S JUST BUSINESS

Losing a job makes you keenly aware that you need to manage your finances. *I wish I had put aside more savings or made better investments so I had more money for this rainy day. If I get another job, then I will manage my money better so that if something ever happens again I will be okay financially.* It takes something like being downsized to shock you into doing things you should have spent more time doing.

I was open to learning more about finances and investment ideas. A free investment show with many free financial seminars was being held in my city. Having the spare time, I decided to attend. It was an excellent decision.

I attended several lectures and workshops, visited booths, and picked up information. *If only I had lots of money to invest.* I came across investments that you could make using money that you had saved in your retirement savings plan—and I came across one that I and my husband decided to do.

Unfortunately, my retirement savings plan was primarily invested in stocks and my stockbroker did not deal in this type of investment. I would have to move a portion of my money over to a retirement savings plan at another institution. My local bank offered the service. I had been with my stockbroker for over twenty years. I first became a client very early in my career and I had asked the investment firm to specifically connect me to a female stockbroker. As a female in a male-dominated profession, I felt that I wanted to support another one. She was also in the early stage of her career. We had built a good relationship over the years.

I had pondered occasionally over the last few years whether I should move my entire account to a self-directed one to avoid the annual management fee, but had always decided to remain with her. Though I could have transferred my entire portfolio to the bank, I decided to keep a portion of it with her. It was probably not the most cost-effective decision, but I stayed partly out of a sense of loyalty and partly so I would still have access to her stock advice. I had made the decision to go ahead with an investment that I believed was sound and beneficial and had offered the opportunity to her first—even though it was more convenient and cheaper for me to deal with my local bank.

It was thus with surprise and disappointment that I received an e-mail from her indicating that she would no longer be managing my account since "the size of our business dictates that we can no longer manage client relationships of this size" and that she could transfer me to another group within the investment company that was run as a "premium call centre" for a portfolio of my size.

For over $130 in annual fees, I could call a call centre if I wanted to sell a stock—and still pay a large commission.

After being in a long-time client relationship, I was let go. This reminded me of my downsizing. Even though I had been with someone a long time and had done my part and paid my fees, it didn't matter. It all revolved around making a profit and what's in it for them. The people equation was gone. My portfolio was so small that she didn't want to manage it anymore—even though I would be paying the full annual fee. She was quick to let me go even though I had been a good client who was not demanding and had followed her recommendations and advice on what to buy and sell over the years.

It is sad that society and business has gone this way. Just like in being downsized—thank you very much for your past services, but business dictates we no longer want you. It has become the norm in business.

I wrote back to tell her that I had decided to move my entire portfolio away from the firm instead of just part. It was a small act of revenge. It was a bitter act. I was truly sorry that this has become the way of the world.

Lessons Learned:

- It's just business. You may believe that you have a relationship with someone you are doing business with, but beware. If you are no longer bringing in as much revenue to them, they may be quick to get rid of you. Their actions are justifiable to them in the name of business.
- You need to manage your own finances. I had left most of my portfolio management to my stockbroker—buying and selling based on her recommendations. There were other investment options available that she didn't deal in—and I was left out

of. You must take an active role in the management of your money.

- Educate yourself financially. If I hadn't decided to learn more about other investment options, I would likely not have found one that suited my needs better. It is good to have diversified investments, especially since the stock market is volatile.

- Attend financial trade shows. Financial trade shows are often held in large cities and often have low or free admission prices. The admission cost is low because they want to attract people to attend so that the various financial companies or organizations can showcase their investment opportunities and perhaps attract new investors. There are often free seminars or workshops that teach you about various topics. It is a good way to get exposure to what is available.

- Do it now. Don't wait until you are downsized to wish you had managed your money better. Do it now. Spend a little time thinking each week about your money and how to grow it— rather than regretting you hadn't when it is too late and you don't have a continuous source of income anymore. What you focus on, improves.

28. SOLDIERING ON

I was soaking up the sun at a local theme park as my kids were off playing in the water. A large roller coaster was silhouetted against the sky. As the roller coaster dove, the screams of the riders rang out.

We usually went to the theme park as a family, but my partner was not there that day. I started thinking about how nice it was that I could be out there on a Monday with the kids, instead of at the office like he was. When I started to think of all the downsizings, the roller coaster dove again and the screams rang out. Only this time instead of screams of happy delight, they cut into me like screams of pain and fear. Over and over they screamed as they rode on the roller coaster, the roller coaster of life. It was the same drop we were plunging through.

I told myself to snap out of it, and forced myself to think happy thoughts, to make the screams happy again. I wanted to enjoy the day. We stayed late into the night. The kids had a great time—I love being with them.

That night, my friend who works for a large company, told me that several people in his department were let go. It would happen every day over the next two or so weeks—approximately 150 people per day.

The following week, I spoke to him again. It had been an awful day. He was on an escalation call (a call held when there is a problem that needs to be escalated higher up in management for resolution). It was called by another on the project team. The person told him he had escalated it because he had a meeting with his boss in forty-five minutes and was likely going to be let go. He wanted to let him know where the project stood and what the issues were before he was gone.

A manager who worked in his office row told him that he was being called in for a meeting with his boss that afternoon—and he believed he would be let go. The manager had packed his laptop, ready to hand in, and went to the meeting. My friend and others had watched him go. He never came back. He was right. He was gone.

Another manager had called to finalize the arrangements for an employee of hers who was transferring to his department. She told him that she had been called in for a meeting with her boss the next day. Since she might not be there any longer, she wanted to make sure she had taken care of everything for her employee before she left. She was looking out for her staff, knowing that she would be gone soon.

Apparently, it was rumored that all the HR folks were worried that it would be their turn once all the others had been done. After all, you wouldn't need as many HR personnel if you have fewer personnel. All the HR folks were sitting in on the downsizing meetings, knowing that at the end of the process, it could be them at the receiving end. It must have been hard to watch someone being informed they no longer have a job and to walk them out, and know that it might be you soon.

Those stories made me see the image of brave people marching off to their duty, still doing their jobs, and scrambling to make sure everything was in order before they left. Hundreds more going to work each day—not knowing if it was their last—and carrying on with their job. I cry at their bravery and honor. It reminds me of how I had wanted to go over that last report of mine with my boss.

On a morning run, I stopped by a house that had its garage door open with a very large pink flamingo on display. It stood almost shoulder high and was quite eye-catching. I admired it and called out my appreciation to the lady beside it. She responded and I stopped to talk to her briefly. When I was about to leave, she mentioned that she was retired but didn't have a pension. I asked her where she had worked, and she replied that she hadn't worked for a few years and that her husband supported them. I confided to her that I had been recently let go. She told me that her brother-in-law had just been let go as well. His company had gone bankrupt and he was left without a job—and no severance pay. His wife's father was very ill and was not expected to live long. The wife did not earn enough money to support the family for long—and they were all under a lot of stress. He was left without anything.

When I continued my run, I thought of him—and realized that I had to write this book for the hundreds of others who were being downsized and felt alone, without any support. Even for those who do—just to let them know that they are not alone in some of their feelings and to help them through the initial period. I wanted to be able to give them some advice and tools to help them get back on their feet.

That weekend I was at a Dragon boat competition. My teammate who had been let go the previous week was still bitter. I told her that time would heal, and she had the opportunity to do something else. Others marveled that other than the initial announcement of her company's downsizings, they had not heard anything else. It was true. Once it was announced, it was news and made headlines. Now it was no longer news—and the execution happened quietly. So it was for all the other large terminations. So it happens to the hundreds of smaller companies not worthy of a news mention. It goes on. The downsizing continues.

I ran by the flamingo house again a few days later. I was reminded that I needed to finish this book and reach out and perhaps help someone in their time of need. I started out writing to express my own thoughts and help myself out of the turmoil; however, this could be a tool to help others in a similar situation. There are so many layoffs and downsizings —and it seems to be a trend. It is almost a commonplace occurrence now.

Later that morning, I received a call from a friend of mine. She told me the names of four recruitment firms that she had been given by a mutual friend. She also told me the names of some of the people we both knew that were now downsized.

Negative announcements were happening everywhere. Hewlett-Packard had bought another company, EDS, and would downsize by about 25,000 workers globally, the largest downsizing ever. A prominent securities firm in the United States, Lehman Brothers, folded. Lehman Brothers had survived the Great Depression and 9/11, but not the sub-prime mortgage crisis now enveloping the US financial sector. Merrill Lynch agreed to sell itself to Bank of America to avert a deepening financial crisis. AIG, one of the largest insurance firms in the world, was being bailed out by the Federal Reserve to avoid a global financial crisis. Greater job losses were expected in the financial sector. Stock markets around the world plummeted. Great Britain had officially gone into recession, which is defined as two consecutive quarters with no growth. Many other countries were on the verge. With a recession, more companies would be in financial trouble and more downsizings would occur. The ripple effects would widen. Meanwhile, I found that a position I had been hoping for had been filled internally by the company.

The American government authorized a $700 billion bail-out of Wall Street in an effort to keep their economy from imploding. The European banks were also in crisis and had formed a bailout package to aid the banks. Global recession was predicted. A large number of jobs were gone—with more to come.

I had hoped that the crisis would be short. Unfortunately, even though we would eventually get through this, downsizing is a part of our society. It will continue everywhere. It is something that we cannot control.

Almost every day there was news of more companies downsizing and laying off workers. Consumer confidence was at a low. General Motors, Ford, and Chrysler were all in serious financial trouble. Without government financial aid, they were in danger of collapsing. The ripple effects of the automakers' troubles were spreading throughout the economy and the government was moving to do what it could to prop it up.

Leading economists were saying that things were likely to get worse before they got better, and that the recession, now confirmed, would last longer than originally thought. Of course, the big D word—Depression, kept popping up. Were we heading into a depression? Would it be as hard and as long as the Great Depression of the thirties? Memories of soup kitchen lines and poverty were striking fear in families. The stock markets continued to plummet, surprising everyone with how quickly it slid.

For some strange reason, I was not afraid. I was not sure why, given all the bad economic news. I still had hope.

I remember the words of an old song that had been a refrain from a television show when I was young:

Que sera, sera
Whatever will be, will be
The future's not ours to see
Que sera, sera
What will be, will be."[16]

I don't know what the future holds for me. I don't know what it holds for the many who are being downsized. Some will do better—some worse. We have no choice but to forge on to weather the storms of the economy and life.

I consider myself one of the lucky ones. My skills and health were good. I had a wonderful family. I was optimistic that eventually I would land some type of job.

The world abounds with stories of those who have endured much worse troubles and have kept faith and triumphed over their circumstances in the end. How you choose to perceive and deal with your circumstances can make a huge difference in how you make it through. You can trek on in misery and spiral down into despair—or take strength and have gratitude for what you have and persevere. What choice would you rather make?

"I got soul, but I'm not a soldier"—these are words from a song[17] in a Nike commercial [18] that was played on television during the 2008 Olympics. It depicted athletes trying their best—some falling, some triumphing—and demonstrating their hope, courage, and tenacity.

I have soul, though I am not a soldier. I will persevere. You will too. We will navigate through whatever life throws us. Take strength in the fact that you are not alone; these times will pass and become a memory. What will be the difference is how we choose to approach what life throws our way. This is our journey—a journey that can take us to new and better places. Keep hope. Keep going.

29. ANOTHER D WORD

The recession continued. Whispers of the D word abounded—inspiring fear and belt-tightening. Companies that were hanging on as long as they could were forced to lay people off. Companies that had already let people go were going through another round. Fear of whether it could lead to a depression. Economists foretold that things would get better in the coming year, but it would be a while before the effects would be seen. Some had said that things would be better by the beginning of the year—now they were saying we might not feel the recovery until much later.

It seemed that they didn't really know. No one had predicted this recession, or how fast things would decline once it began. The governments were spending billions to prop up the economy. Where was this money coming from? I read that in order to pay the debt load, the government was just printing more money. The US had moved away from the gold standard in the seventies—dollars were not backed by gold anymore. Printing lots of money without anything real to back it will only invite inflation. Inflation devalues any savings that you have—unless you have it invested in something that will keep up with it.

I read an anecdote about a lady who, during a period of hyperinflation, went to a bakery to buy some bread. She brought a wheelbarrow full of paper money to pay for the bread, and left it outside momentarily as she went in to get the storekeeper. When she came out, thieves had made off with the wheelbarrow but left behind the money. The wheelbarrow was worth more than the money, which was useless paper and could not purchase much.

My mother told me about inflation—and how it was better to buy something that they could use, rather than hang onto money that would become devalued such that they couldn't buy the same item with it anymore. She had experienced it—and imparted some lessons from hard times.

Another childhood memory was one of being shown some old Chinese paper money. The denominations were in the thousands and I was suitably awed—until my mother told me it was only worth a few cents in Canadian money. When I was young, an ice cream cone only cost ten cents. It costs more than twenty times that now. I have seen inflation creeping up over the years. Inflation can be a silent thief, taking away your purchasing power.

I considered my own situation. Should I invest in something tangible? I was not working—I couldn't afford to spend my money on anything unless I absolutely needed it. But if I didn't invest, my money might become devalued. Such is life. Once you don't have something, you wish you had taken better care of it when you had the chance.

I vowed to review my savings—primarily in registered retirement savings plans—to see if there was something better I should invest in. I was disheartened to learn that the stocks in my retirement savings plans had already taken a nosedive. To sell anything I had would solidify the paper loss that I currently had—and I was hoping it would recover on its own.

It's a shame that it usually takes a tragedy to shock us into wanting to do the right things that we should have been doing all along.

We have become a consumer society—happy to spend in the belief that the money would keep flowing in to support our habits. Statistics show that the average family has net negative savings. The generation that lived through the Great Depression knew the value of saving. This generation will perhaps be scared back into it. My generation. My generation is facing the D word. Depression … depression of the economy … depression of the mind.

It is hard to keep from being depressed. D. Dejected, destitute, debilitated, devalued, demoralized, death.

Enough of this, I decided. D can also be delightful, daring, delicious, divine, determined, and decisive. Yes, determined and decisive. From then on, I decided I was determined to do better.

Many people experienced huge losses with the stock market declines. The large cohort of baby boomers facing retirement—the most affected by a current loss in value of their stocks—are lamenting their potentially ruined comfortable retirement. Stocks have been climbing back recently. I was hopeful that this trend would continue, though this could be a case of false, flailing flutters as it bounces inexorably down, downsizing others along its way.

Lessons Learned:

- Inflation is a silent thief that takes away your purchasing power. Have your money invested in things that will keep pace with inflation.
- Keep an eye on your savings and investments and make sure that you have them in the most appropriate things for your stage in life. If you are close to retirement, don't have most of your money in stocks that you could lose and not have time to recover.
- The experts don't always know what will happen. They were caught by surprise by the sudden economic collapse. It is up to you to take a common sense approach to your finances and to always be prepared in case something unexpected happens.
- Be determined to manage your money well all the time— rather than waiting until it is too late. There is no time like the present.

30. THE HURT NEVER GOES AWAY

You feel the blood rushing to your head, your heart pounding. Even though it's happened before to me, being in sales it happens quite often, you still feel it—the blood rushing to your head as they tell you. When you realize what is happening. That was the description an acquaintance used to describe how he felt after being told he was being downsized.

I can recall the image of him describing it—I felt the agony of the moment—and the realization of what was happening.

Downsizing was not the topic of the conversation that night. It was actually a discussion on reactions and emotions among a group of us. The example came spontaneously and was used as an example that he thought others would understand easily. It caught me by surprise though I did not show it.

I was fine and was over my own downsizing, but the words brought the memories rushing to the surface. I immediately identified with it. I felt empathy toward him as I shared in his pain, though he was oblivious to it.

When I was downsized a former co-worker told me that the pain of getting downsized is never easier—no matter how many times you have gone through it. You just bounce back quicker each time. Yes, it can happen several times, but the pain never goes away. It still hurts.

This was the first time I had ever been downsized. It may not be my last. I am saddened by the thought of all those who have also gone through it, knowing that I am in good company, knowing that there were many, many, more before me, and many, many more to come. It is a sad fact of life—and there is always the fear that it could happen again. No matter what you do and how good you may be, you could just be in the wrong place at the wrong time. We have become a society used to its common presence.

Plus we all have our little faults. We go through the introspection and self-questioning. Why did they pick me? What did I do wrong? We begin to question and doubt our abilities. We begin to lose self-confidence. The hurt never goes away.

What can we do about it? It will always be with us. The trick is to not dwell on it and to move on. Take steps in another direction.

There are newspaper accounts and movies made of people who are laid off and who have become so embittered they seek revenge. Why? Because they are hurt. Because the hurt doesn't go away. Because they have let it consume them.

This is the danger of the downsized ones. This is the tragedy of the downsized. The hurt never goes away. Don't let it consume you because it does you no good.

Realize it. Know it. Accept it. Pick yourself up and upsize yourself. Take comfort in the fact that you are not alone. Then move on.

You must.

Lessons Learned:

- The hurt never goes away. Accept it and move on.
- Dwelling on your downsizing only makes matters worse. What you focus on can take on greater proportions. The negativity will colour your interactions with others and make it harder to promote yourself and appear confident in your job search. Don't let it consume you and make you depressed or crazy.
- Don't self-incriminate. What has happened, has happened. It could happen again. Think about how you might do things differently next time—and take it as a learning experience. Don't get stuck in the past.
- It does get easier. As time passes, the tasks of the present fill my mind and the thoughts of my downsizing decrease. Time is a healer and the path to upsizing yourself.
- Share your experience. I was grateful to know what others had experienced so I could know what to expect. To know that the hurt is always there and to be mentally prepared. Maybe for the next time? I hope not. But at least I am more prepared.

31. PERSEVERANCE

Perseverance. Looking for a job is a full-time job. At a networking support group, they said, "Don't forget to smile and have fun!" They meant it to remind us to not let the stress of not having a job get to us. Someone near me told us that–when this statement had been said the week before—someone had burst out, "Fun? I don't have time to have fun! I need to be serious and spend my time seriously looking for a job!" Obviously the stress had been getting to him. Obviously he wasn't having fun.

I felt guilty hearing this. I was not spending the same amount of time on my job search as this man was. He would likely get a job before me because he was desperate. I didn't feel as desperate. Perhaps I should. I could use the push to keep me at it. I needed more drive to succeed and intense motivation. I needed to push myself, but I hated it. I hated my situation. I hated applying and hoping and not hearing. I didn't want to do it, but I knew I had to.

My days filled up rapidly. I was not doing a full-time job search. I tried to discipline myself to do it first thing in the morning after the kids left for school. I settled on a slightly more than half-day schedule. I searched until an early lunch around 11:30, and then searched again until 1:00. After that, I seemed to have a multitude of other errands, chores, and things to do. I would have thought that I would have time to read, reflect, and work on projects that I had always wanted to do but never had time for before, but I still didn't seem to have that much more time.

"Why not?" I asked myself. "Am I wasting my time? No, I am as busy as ever—just differently."

They say things expand to fill your available time. It was true. I picked up my daughter and drove her home from school every day. If I was working, she would have taken the bus. The school is only a ten-minute drive from our home, but it's a one-hour trip involving two buses and a ten-minute walk if she took public transportation. It was not very pleasant, particularly in inclement weather. Of course, being a loving parent, I opted to pick her up.

I cooked more from scratch, creating healthier, less expensive meals. I enjoyed the results. These results took time.

We ate less on the run and in the car on the way to the kids' sports training. It was nicer and more relaxed. This took time.

I shopped around more, saving us money by buying groceries and other items at the best price at different locations. This took time.

I was able to keep my house tidier. This took time.

What about when I go back to work? I wouldn't have time anymore.

If I wanted a job, though, I needed to keep at it. Perseverance. It's a numbers game. If I don't apply, I certainly won't get it. If the chances are low, then I need to get myself out there more. Don't get sidetracked. Don't get too busy with other things.

Perseverance is the key. I must persevere. The only way to upsize yourself is to persevere. I knew this, but knowledge does not always translate into action. However, it is action that brings results.

Lessons Learned:

- Looking for a job is a full-time job. You need to spend time to get results.
- Perseverance is the key. Even though the economy might be bad and there aren't many jobs available, you must persevere. If you don't apply, you won't get anything.
- Be careful not to get too busy doing other things with your newfound time. Keep your focus on your job search.

32. I'VE LANDED

I've landed! I've landed! I've landed! I've landed. This is the term that my networking group used when someone has obtained a job. It conjured up images of a plane or rocket ship coming in successfully to a landing. I liked the sound of it. It felt safe.

It was my turn now. I'd made it. I started in three weeks. I'd landed. I found it entirely on my own. I'd responded to a job position and sent in my resume. They called me in for an interview. I was interviewed a second time and was offered a position. It just goes to show that you can sometimes find a job the traditional way.

My networking group met once a week. When someone landed a job, they were to go up in front of everyone to tell them about it. The idea behind this was to let the rest know that success is possible and could be around the corner.

Usually the speaker was upbeat, telling of how he or she had landed that particular job and how they may have encountered many hurdles and rejections before. I did find it motivating to know that people were getting jobs and had faced rejection many times before landing one.

I pondered what I would say. I wanted to give some words of encouragement. Or I could simply just stop going. I owed them nothing. I had paid a membership fee to belong. I had been downsized over a year ago now. It was time to move on.

Hi my name is … I've landed. The job … description … I found it by … and this is what I will be doing now.

When I arrived that day, I told the convener that I had landed. I brought two boxes of Timbits, the little round doughnuts from Tim Horton's, a coffee and doughnuts store, to share and celebrate with the others as was customary with the group. When I arrived, I saw that there were some Timbit boxes there already. Someone else had landed too. They had said in the past few weeks that the job market was getting better and more jobs were available. It appeared we were evidence of this fact. In fact, there were three of us that day.

Going up to speak is voluntary, but highly encouraged by the organizers. It is, after all, good news …a happy ending…a safe landing after being cut loose and left to wander searching for another berth.

I let the other two speak first, describing their new positions and how they found them. When it was my turn, I made my way from the back of the room to the front and took the microphone. I started off with the usual spiel by introducing myself, my background, and my new job. They clapped dutifully. They thought it was over. Then I spoke some more.

"It took me a while before I recovered. I looked for jobs, but halfheartedly. I didn't really want to go back right away. I hid behind the recession. I blamed the lack of finding a job due to the recession, when truthfully I was not looking as hard as I might have been.

"How do you explain to an employer why there is such a large gap between when you were laid off and when you are now being interviewed and finding a job? Why was it taking you so long to get a job? The unanswered question being in their minds 'Is there something wrong with you that we don't know about? Something that makes other employers not want to hire you?'

"I was off for a long time. At first I wasn't sure how to explain it to prospective employers without sounding as if I didn't want to work. I decided upon a simple, straightforward answer that seemed to work well—after all it was the truth. 'My company had a downsizing and I was laid-off after being with them for many years. I took some time off and stayed home and spent time with my family, and now I am ready to go back to work.' The upbeat, ready-to-go answer made me sound re-energized by my stay home—my long rest a benefit to the new employers, rather than a handicap.

"So to all of you who may be worrying about being out of the workforce a long time, here is an answer that may also apply to you. I wish all of you the best of luck in finding something eventually."

My speech over, I went back to my seat. At the break, many people came up to me, including one of the organizers, to confide that they had taken it hard when they were laid off and couldn't do any searching at all at first. They all appreciated my story and my words of encouragement.

I realized how many had identified with me as I suspected, and were keeping their feelings hidden at these meetings as they tried to move on and go through the proper motions of job searching, blaming themselves for not searching harder—but not really wanting to wade back into the work force yet. Wanting the break, but deep down worrying about the impacts of a prolonged absence. Berating themselves for their lack of drive, but at the same time unable to motivate themselves to try harder, not knowing how to mentally upsize themselves. Fearful of the consequences the longer they were adrift.

My story and words gave them encouragement. They were not the only ones. I was a prime example of someone who landed after a prolonged absence. They could too. It was just a matter of time and being ready to go back again. Of rightsizing themselves by being prepared mentally and having the right tools and job search techniques at hand.

I have rightsized myself. I have landed.

Lessons Learned:

- Many people find it hard to get back into the workforce right away after being downsized. If you have been at a company for a long time, losing employment there can be quite an impact mentally. It is important to realize that this is common and you are not the only one.

- If it has been a long time since you were laid off—and it is because you took a break—a simple answer for prospective employers is that you are now ready to go back to work. It is honest—and is a positive response indicating that you are ready to move forward now.

- Don't be afraid to let others know. I wasn't sure if I should speak up and admit to others how I delayed finding a job, but I was glad that I did. It was positive encouragement to many others who were ashamed or fearful of not being driven to find work right away, when they felt that is what they should be doing and what others expected of them.

- Don't feel bad for wanting to take a break. It is normal. Give yourself some time. You will begin to slowly rightsize yourself as you get mentally ready.

- Stay positive. You will land.

33. A COMMENTARY ON DOWNSIZING TODAY

Downsizing is commonplace—even when revenues are fine. It has become a standard profitability tool. Downsizing is restructuring for greater profitability, business engineering. We have become accustomed to it. It is almost an everyday occurrence in good times or bad. It just occurs even greater in bad.

It is a cause for concern when someone can speak so casually about having being downsized several times and everyone accepts this statement as a norm in today's world.

What kind of environment and society are we creating? What kind of loyalty to a company do we inspire?

They say that the average employee will work for several companies over their lifetime now and that the time spent at any company will be an average of two years. How do you gain in-depth experience in a company to be able to contribute effectively then?

In the past, leaders of companies were typically long-term employees who had risen through the ranks. They had great depth of knowledge and experience in their company's business that was respected and desired. This is often not the case today. It is rare, unless it is a privately owned family company.

Can one gain enough knowledge and experience about a specific company's business to be able to make a legacy contribution? Will more mistakes and inefficiencies be made now through inexperience? Is there much loyalty to a company from their employees if those employees have not been with them for long—and they know that they are expendable? Whose primary concern is to their own future and not necessarily that of their company?

Many corporate executives are on renewable contracts. If the performance of the company during their current term is not good, then their contract may not be renewed. This promotes a short-term view by those who are running our companies. There is no incentive to implement long-term plans that might not bring immediate benefit and could cost more to the bottom line in the short term, since to do well now is what becomes important.

It becomes very important to constantly show a profit. If revenues drop, then the quick solution is to cut expenses. Salaries are often the largest and easiest expense to cut. The average loaded cost of an employee (salary, benefits, administrative, and physical overhead) can easily run $100,000 per year or more. Cut ten people, save a million dollars right there.

In a recent newspaper article[19], the impacts of the housing meltdowns and joblessness in America are dismaying. Social researchers are only just beginning to assess the human toll. The article mentions that the Pew Research Center has been studying some of the effects and has noted that what is especially striking is:

> The sense of permanence that has settled in among some Americans who've suffered the most—middle-class, middle-income, middle-aged Americans, especially baby boomers in the 59–64 age bracket, many of whom have burned through all their assets and now face a retirement under unchangeably diminished circumstances.
>
> This translates to psychological impacts. Four out of ten of the unemployed we spoke to tell us family relations have suffered, 40 percent said they lost contact with close friends. And a third say they have lost self-respect.

Staggering results—40 percent losing contact with close friends? They are no doubt cocooning, hiding away from the world, finding it difficult to face others.

Loss of self-respect? This is the mental anguish of not being able to provide for your family anymore. Not feeling good enough to have been kept on at their company.

The article went on to say that many have rethought their careers in the downward sense, settling for and making do with jobs that just aren't as good as what they had.

I believe this will have significant impacts to our society going forward. Even when individuals are able to upsize themselves and get another job, their view on work and life has changed. There is no loyalty to a company that you know will cut you in the blink of an eye if the company feels it will help their profits. Stress levels among workers are high and people work longer hours out of fear that they may lose their jobs. Their health is at risk. Their immediate boss may be sympathetic, but they are powerless when the downsizing orders come from higher above. Turnover will be higher and we are already seeing this effect.

What about the children of these families who see parents who have worked hard all of their lives—only to be gotten rid of so easily despite their experience and many years with the company? Are we creating a generation of cynical workers whose only concern is for themselves and who readily hop jobs for the promise of something better? Who don't really care if they leave suddenly because everyone does? This will affect how well a company can manage.

What about those executives who make those decisions? The ones who know that, if they don't meet their annual revenue targets, they may be out the door themselves? They have lost the feeling for the affected employees. It has become a financial exercise in planning sessions as one of the options to meet profitability targets. Just the other day, a major company announced an increase in their third quarter and year-over-year profits, when earlier that year a quiet slew of cuts to the workforce had occurred. A friend had survived the cuts in his department there.

When I first began my career, downsizing was an option of last resort that happened when a company was facing bankruptcy or would not be able to pay the salaries of the employees they had. It was a survival option and one taken with great regret. Great attempts were taken to avoid it. As more companies downsized, it became more acceptable.

Instead of being an option of last resort, it has become a tool to help increase profits—even when the company is doing well. Restructuring or reengineering the organization of the company and being able to work with fewer people is looked upon by many as a smart and sensible move, helping the company to greater profitability and enabling it to better compete pricewise.

According to an analysis by the Associated Press using data provided by Equilar, an executive compensation research firm, the typical pay package for the head of a US company in the Standard & Poor's 500 was $9 million in 2010.[20] CEO's at the largest companies in the US were paid better in 2010 than they were in 2007 when the economy was growing and unemployment was roughly half what it is today. It is as if the recession didn't happen.

In Canada, the results are similar. Canada's best-paid chief executives also waltzed through the recession with average earnings of $6 million in 2009 which is 155 times higher than the average Canadian income of $40,500, according to a study by the Canadian Centre for Policy Alternatives.[21] Compare this to 1998 when CEOs received an average of 104 times more than the average Canadian income. We can see that the compensation gap between executives and the average worker is increasing at an alarming rate. This difference is even more pronounced in the United States.

It is quite understandable and reasonable to give those who have the skills and abilities to lead our companies a much higher compensation than the average employee. Executives typically put in long hours, have a specialized skill set that may have taken years to develop, and are often put in demanding, stressful positions. Yes, I agree that they should earn more. Are they really worth over 100 times more though? Are they 155 times better than the average person? Ten to twenty times maybe. One hundred? Not. Certainly not even higher as the trend appears to be going.

Boards of companies argue that to attract and retain top talent, they must offer higher compensation. I would argue that this is more of an ego-satisfying mechanism for the executives whose egos and sense of self-worth are gratified at being able to command such high prices for their services. They could live quite comfortably on a few hundred thousand dollars annually. It is more the satisfaction of being able to command millions annually that incent them, and as it becomes a norm to compensate at these levels, it becomes a self-perpetuating mechanism which will spiral up out of control. After all, isn't it executives and the wealthy that often sit on corporate boards and benefit from higher average compensation?

CEOs of companies who are able to operate their companies profitably and have lowered cost by getting rid of people are seen as management stars. They are seen as the ones who can be brought in to make the tough decisions.

Several years ago, there was an executive sent by our corporate headquarters into the business unit I was in at the time. He made no secret of the fact that he was given instructions to observe the operations of our unit and make recommendations. These included getting rid of people, including our VPs and Directors and the business unit head too, if warranted in his opinion. After several months, he cleaned shop. Gone was our VP of sales. Gone were several directors. Gone were many others. Gone in the name of business. An accepted norm. One repeated in many companies all over. Gone in the name of making sound business decisions.

Are they really sound business decisions? It has gotten to the point where cuts are so deep in companies that the remaining employees are overworked and many things are falling to the wayside. One person said, "There are so many balls that I'm juggling that I am just trying to catch them and hope that they don't fall." Will a company be able to plan and do their best—or are they just busy trying to meet the immediate demands of the day with the limited resources they now have on hand?

What about the hidden costs to the companies and our health care system from the results of stress? What about the loss in knowledge and experience?

It could end up costing the company far more in the long run by letting go of experienced, skilled personnel that the company has invested years of training in, than the short-term gain obtained by removing them. Instead, you have more mistakes made from inexperience—and more things undone by those who don't know how to do it.

The decision to go with a cheaper solution may do fine for now, but could eventually cause more problems long term. But that's acceptable to our decision makers because the future will be someone else's problem to deal with. Their job is to do things as cheaply as possible today.

The ones who have a conscience—the ones who try to do things the right way regardless of cost— don't last. They are pushed aside by someone who can increase the profits.

The cost to individuals, families, and society of constant downsizings—and a lack of stability—invariably leads to a self-centered and hardened approach. There is a widening split between those who have jobs and those who don't.

There are even movies created with downsizing as the theme, such as *The Company Men* or *Up in the Air*.

Linda Barnard of *The Toronto Star* reviewed *The Company Men:*

> Seeing people trudge to the elevator with packed boxes, tearful goodbyes, anger, and sorrow are as much a part of the pattern of working life today as Gene musing he's worth half a million more than he was when he woke up that morning. Layoffs bring a rise in stock prices that will protect the company, and isn't that why GTX is doing it?[22]

The fear is palpable and one of the reasons for the continued recession. Even those with jobs are afraid to spend in case they are downsized. With less goods being purchased, companies tighten their belts more and let more people go, and the downward spiral continues.

Each company, by downsizing to increase their profitability, in the end indirectly hurts themselves in the long run because those they have downsized no longer have the money to purchase the products that are being sold. Of course, the company's rationale is that the company's costs are reduced.

One might argue that if you guarantee a person employment, then they will not be motivated to perform as well. There are other motivators, however, such as profit-sharing, recognition, or growth opportunities that can be used to incent the right behavior. Studies have also shown that salary is not the number-one driver amongst employees. If people are motivated to perform, they will do so. The trick is to find the right motivating forces.

In the not-so-distant past, it was the norm for women not to have the right to vote, and for people to smoke cigarettes wherever they chose. It was thought of as perfectly acceptable. Now the times and laws have changed and we look back at those times and see how wrong they were and that women should be able to vote, and that smoking is not healthy and should not be allowed to affect others. Perhaps, in the future, we will look back and see rampant downsizing as a social wrong that we cannot comprehend why we engaged in it to the detriment of our society.

In his national bestselling book, *Empire of Illusion*,[23] Pulitzer Prize-winner Chris Hedges discussed the dire state of North America. Consumers are $14 trillion in debt. A loss of a job can easily lead to bankruptcy and loss of home. The government has been borrowing or printing new money and nobody knows how the government will ever be able to pay these loans back.

He writes of how the masses are being placated by illusions and do not realize the state we are in. It is an illuminating and thought-provoking book and I highly recommend it. It is a wakeup call to what is happening around us.

Economic turmoil brings political instability. Witness the unrest sweeping through the Middle East. At the heart of it is the ability of the common person to adequately take care of their family. Countries worldwide are in economic crisis. Political turmoil will surface domestically as people lash out in frustration. The Occupy Wall Street movement is a symptomatic outcry.

So what can we do about this? Perhaps one way is to start saying collectively to stop downsizing for profit reasons only. If a company is making money, then it should be socially unacceptable for them to downsize employees. Maybe we should stop investing in companies that downsize for profit only. Some people only buy ethical stocks or funds that specialize in green initiatives. Why not invest in those companies that have publicly stated goals that they will only downsize as a last resort when revenues are negative?

There are slogans such as "Buy American," or "Made in Canada." Taking care of our own or being a growing company are ideals to aspire to. That will inspire loyalty and draw good employees. We could recognize companies who retain a lot of people and have low turnovers. Social recognition is good for business and can inspire companies to behave in a way to gain it. Fair trade coffee is an example of where consumers will pay more for coffee that is produced ethically, and who will boycott those that do not.

Without enough hue and cries over the long-term impacts, things will continue as they are. The green environmental movement has gained momentum from people who have spoken up. Companies are now more environmentally conscious and will spend the money and time to ensure that they are being environmentally responsible. They promote the fact that they are doing this. How about social responsibility? How about creating an environment where companies are proud of the fact that they have good retention of their employees and strive toward this?

We need to become people responsible now. How about saying no to constant downsizing and saying yes to stability? Let's grow so we utilize our people. How about finding ways to keep people gainfully employed rather than how to do without them?

Gary Hawton is a key player in a movement to give Canadian shareholders a say in the compensation given to CEOs. According to the Vancouver-based Shareholder Association for Research and Education (SHARE), forty-five companies have agreed to give shareholders non-binding votes on CEO pay packages. In 2010, 27 companies held a vote. The biggest dissatisfaction was at Barrick Gold where 13.7 percent voted against the recommended pay package. In 2009, Barrick's CEO topped the Top 100 CEO pay list with $24.2 million in compensation.[24] Movements like this are headed in the right direction. Public and shareholder pressure must be brought to bear so that more companies follow this path.

We are in a new age where individuals, via the Internet, have more power to affect change. Facebook and Twitter can bring pressure and spark social outrage caused by individuals posting news that can go viral, reaching thousands almost instantaneously. We have seen this from numerous examples—most notably from the uprisings in the Middle East that were sparked by regular citizens posting pictures and messages online that incited and directed the population to rise up in protest against their governments.

Don Tapscott and Anthony Williams, the authors of the best seller *Wikinomics: How Mass Collaboration Changes Everything*,[25] give numerous examples of the way the world is changing due to the presence of the Internet. They inform of how the Internet allows mass or global collaboration that is changing how our economies are influenced.

A wiki is a website that allows visitors to make changes, contributions, or corrections.[26] The most recognized example of it in use is Wikipedia, an online encyclopedia that is created collaboratively by multiple people contributing content. It demonstrates how people from all over the world can together create something that is more extensive than what any one encyclopedia company on its own could have produced.

According to the front flap overview in Tapscott and Williams' latest book, *Macrowikinomics: Rebooting Business and the World*:[27]

In every corner of the globe, a powerful new model of economic and social innovation is sweeping across all sectors—one where people with drive, passion, and expertise take advantage of new Web-based tools to get more involved in making the world more prosperous, just, and sustainable.

Tapscott and Williams show that in more than a dozen fields—from finance to health care, science to education, the media to the environment—we have reached a historic turning point: cling to the old industrial era paradigms or use collaborative innovation to revolutionize not only the way we work, but how we live, learn, create, govern, and care for one another.

We have the tools to take action.

I caution that this must be done in a thoughtful way, with well thought out avenues of direction, otherwise we could impact our economy and make things worse. Violence and rioting are not the answer.

Jack Layton, a Canadian politician, wrote a letter to all Canadians three days before passing away from cancer on August 22nd, 2011. In it he wrote,

Canada is a great country, one of the hopes of the world. We can be a better one – a country of greater equality, justice and opportunity. We can build a prosperous economy – a society that shares its benefits more freely...

My friends, love is better than anger. Hope is better than fear. Optimism is better than despair. So let us be loving, hopeful and optimistic. And we'll change the world.

These are very inspiring words. Though I have different political ideologies than Jack Layton, this transcends across ideologies and applies to many other countries and peoples. I found it inspirational and a call to action. We can be better. We can be loving, hopeful and optimistic and work towards a better place. Jack Layton believed in this and so do I. We can each do a little bit in our own way to make our world a better place, for ourselves, and for those generations after us. Changes throughout history are made by the efforts of various people.

I have been back to work for over a year now. It was difficult to complete this book once I started working again, with all the demands of a busy work and family life. It would have been easy to say it was something that was nice to do when I had more time, but now I have other priorities that I need to meet. However, I felt that writing this book was necessary to provide—not a textbook how-to approach for those who are job searching—a human perspective and emotional support for others going through job loss. It was also necessary to make others think about what is happening around us. The completion of this book demonstrates that many things can be accomplished if you just keep working at it a bit at a time.

I have presented many comments and questions to ponder. Perhaps with more and more people thinking of solutions and working toward them, we can change the path we have taken and change it to make our world a stronger, more stable place for us all—not only for us, but for our children after us. To start a groundswell of action, people need to say, "Stop! Let's do something about this!" The world is changing. It is up to us to influence it in the direction we want—or we may find it is too late and we are powerless and are just struggling to survive.

The way to eat an elephant is one bite at a time. These are some thoughts to chew on.

Lessons Learned:

- There are many psychological impacts associated with downsizing. Family relations suffering, loss of friends, and loss of self-respect.
- We have the power to make changes. If enough people in society speak up against something, others will listen. If not, we are heading down a sad path for future generations.
- We have the tools to take action. The advent of the Internet and social media have given people the tools to collaborate and influence collectively. We must do it wisely, however, or we could impact the economy and make matters worse.
- We can overcome challenges. Keep working at it.
- *My friends, love is better than anger. Hope is better than fear. Optimism is better than despair. So let us be loving, hopeful and optimistic. And we'll change the world.*
  Jack Layton

TOOLBOX:
Tips and Thoughts

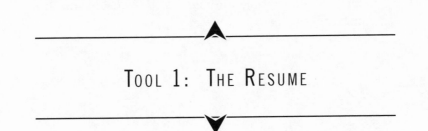

TOOL 1: THE RESUME

The resume is a summary of your work history and background. It is an introduction to you and presents your qualifications so that a prospective employer can quickly ascertain whether they wish to make contact with you. It is a very important document in your job search.

Most resume writing advice suggests that you keep your resume to two pages in length. This I did. However, a friend of mine told me that while the first two pages of her resume followed the standard two-page format—she also included an additional six pages detailing the significant amount of volunteer work that she had done. She was looking for a position in a non-profit sector, but had worked in the corporate sector and felt it was important to bring these aspects out. While I personally think six pages might be a bit too much for an initial contact, you might want to consider adding additional information if you think it is particularly relevant to what you are applying for.

There are resume-writing websites such as www.rockportinstitute.com or www.resume-resource.com , where you can learn how to organize a professional resume and download templates. You can also find resume writing information on job posting sites such as workopolis.ca or monster.ca, along with lots of other job search advice.

For industry specific resume samples and tips check out http://resume.monster.ca or do an Internet search.

Lessons Learned:

- Keep the resume to two pages in length. Any longer gets too detailed. Be succinct and catch their attention with the major items. Save the finer details for the interview.
- Ensure you include all your contact information.

- Use action words. These demonstrate how you were involved.
- Never list your references on the resume. Have your reference list with you at the interview.
- There are numerous websites available to aid you in writing a resume (e.g. www.rockportinsitute.com , www.resume-resource.com, www.workopolis.ca, www.monster.ca).

Tool 2: The Cover Letter

The cover letter is very important. It is likely the first sample of your work the employer will see and use to form an opinion about you. Your written communication provides you with an opportunity to convey your personality and style, and summarize why you are a good candidate for the position.

Your ideas, choice of words, and phrases can help you stand out from the crowd.

As for any standard letter, it should have an opening, middle, and closing. It should not be more than one page. Too much and you are being too wordy. If you are too wordy, it will seem less businesslike and professional. What you want to do is to catch their attention and make them want to interview you.

In the opening, identify who referred you or how you heard of the position. Show interest in the person or company.

In the middle paragraphs, make clear your purpose for writing and the relevance of one or two of your following to the organization: work experience, skills, education, abilities, technical training, and interests. Give proof by stating one or two relevant accomplishments.

You can also show your awareness of some of the types of things the company is doing or wants to achieve. This demonstrates your interest in the company.

In the closing paragraph, indicate your willingness to meet with the employer and say how or when you may be contacted.

The cover letter should always be tailored to the position. Identify how your background and skills match the requirements of this particular job.

Again, the Internet is a good source for samples and advice. Check out www.workopolis.ca or www.monster.ca

I wrote all my own cover letters and resumes. During my job search, an old friend told me that she had hired a professional writer to do her cover letters. She felt that the writer was able to pick out her qualifications and portray her better. However, it was quite costly at a few hundred dollars each. My friend was looking for an executive position and thought it was money well spent for the types of positions she was looking for.

These resources are available if you are not comfortable doing your own resume and cover letters. Prices will vary, depending upon where you go to have it done. Check your local listings, career centres, or ask around for a good source. You can also order cover letters and resumes written for you online with varying prices. The Internet has several providers.

Lessons Learned:

- Keep it to one typewritten page.
- Have an opening paragraph, middle paragraphs, and a closing paragraph as outlined above.
- Tailor each cover letter to each position. Don't use a standard one for every job you apply to.
- Try to address the letter to a specific person.
- If you were referred, mention the referral or where you saw or heard about the position.
- Tell them how you best fit the position. Give proof. Catch their attention.
- Check for spelling, punctuation, or grammar mistakes. Mistakes reflect on you.
- Indicate that you are enclosing your resume.
- Request an interview. Don't be shy—it's standard. Employers expect that you want one anyway, so indicate that you are available and willing to meeting with them at their convenience.
- Sign the letter.
- Outside resources can be hired to write your resume and cover letters for you. These can be expensive.
- The Internet is full of examples and advice.

Tool 3: Your References List

Good references are extremely helpful in your job search. Three to five references, both professional and personal are generally recommended. Prepare a one-page list with all their contact information.

A nice format that I used was to list the reference, title, and contact info, then to give a brief description of how you the reference was related to you (i.e. your previous boss, co-worker, client, long-time friend, etc).

After you have accepted a job, you should thank all your references and network to thank them for their time, assistance, and support.

You should also keep in touch throughout your new career. You may need them again. Also, you might be able to return the favor one day.

Lessons Learned:

- Have several references (three to five), both professional and personal.
- Before listing people as references, check with them that they are willing.
- Make sure you have asked your references whether it is all right to contact them at work or at home.
- Use influential people as references only if they can speak firsthand about you and know you well enough to answer questions about you.
- Telephone your references if you know that they will be contacted by a potential employer. This is considerate so that they will not be surprised. Explain the job fit so that your reference will be prepared.

- When you have accepted a new job, thank your references for their time and support.
- Keep in touch. You never know what can happen in the future.

Tool 4: The Business Card

A simple and handy tool to have in a job search is a personal business card. You might say, "But I don't work for a company anymore! I don't have a job title!" My answer is you do not need one to have a business card. In fact they are great for personal use when you quickly need to give someone your contact info.

The business card can simply state your name, mailing address, e-mail address, and phone number.

It makes you look professional, and provides the receiver with all the information they need to contact you in an easy and acceptable format. Many people will store a business card for future reference, but will potentially misplace something on a piece of paper that you give them.

When my family was at a camp and we were exchanging contact info with another family, I was able to hand over my card to them rather than writing all the information out.

You can easily purchase blank cards at a local office supply store or even places such as Wal-Mart, and print your own at home. This is what I did. There were different colours and styles to choose from. Some were plain white, some had raised embossed outlines or different textures, some had colour backgrounds, such as flowers or cards on them, etc. Choose the one that best suits you and reflects what you want to portray.

To design your card, there are many software templates available that are very simple to use. You can select from pre-made templates where all you need to do is enter your particulars and then print. There were so many styles to choose from—this posed the greatest challenge for me. Once I decided, entering the info and printing was simple.

If you are not comfortable making your own, many small print shops can easily produce them for you.

Another great source is the Internet. You can order free business cards through the online site www.vistaprint.ca

The advantages of having a business card is that, aside from looking very professional, it is a simple and easy tool for giving out your contact information. I recommend having a business card as a useful tool.

Lessons Learned:

- You can easily make your own business cards. Blank cards can be purchased at local office supply stores. You can design and print them yourself on your home computer.
- Free business cards can be designed and ordered online at www.vistaprint.ca.
- Business cards look professional and are an easy way to give out your contact information to prospective employers.
- You can use business cards for personal situations. From now on, I intend to always have a personal card.

TOOL 5: THE 90-SECOND INTRO

First impressions count. It is these critical first moments when you first meet someone—a contact, an interviewer, a potential employer—that you want to convey your message in a clear, succinct manner. Hence, the 90-second intro.

In these ninety seconds, you want to be able to articulate who you are and what it is that you are looking for. The structure consists of a quick overview of your past experience, followed by why you are looking for a new opportunity, and what you are interested in doing next. You finish with an open-ended question that they cannot answer with a yes or no:

> I am a business analyst with x years of experience with a major pharmaceutical company in a strategic planning, analytical, and management role. My company recently downsized, and as result I am now pursuing other opportunities. I am interesting in pursuing a similar position in the x area. I would enjoy hearing your reactions on how your company is handling the recent launch of your new product x.

Having a prepared introduction not only saves you time thinking of what to say when you first meet, but it also allows you to encapsulate all the pertinent information that you would like to convey and sets the stage for further conversation. You do not want to start rambling about your life story at the very beginning, but should be brief and to the point and let the conversation carry from there.

Lessons Learned:

- Have a prepared 90-second introduction. It should consist of an overview of your past experience, why you are looking for a new opportunity, what you are looking to do next. Finish with an open-ended question.
- Rehearse it aloud. Try it out on friends. You want to be natural at saying it.

Tool 6: Your Marketing Profile

Through a meeting at a networking session, I was introduced to the concept of having a marketing profile. This is a summary page that outlines who you are, your job goals, your main skills, and what industries or companies you are targeting.

It differs from your resume in that it is not as formal. It is like a marketing flyer about you and what type of job you are looking for. It is something that you can give to your friends and contacts to provide them with this type of information—or use it on your own to identify how you are planning to market yourself and what areas you are targeting.

One variation that I saw that I quite liked was by a young technical writer. She definitely knew how to write a nice flyer. She had a professional one-page flyer with her photograph in one corner and was printed in colour on 8" x 11" glossy paper. It was placed on the left side of a folder. On the right side was her resume.

On her marketing profile, in different sections outlined in boxes, she emphasized her job goals, skills, areas of expertise, and a little about herself (e.g. her hobbies and affiliations). It was certainly eye-catching and differentiated her.

This might not be appropriate for you, depending on the type of company or person you are dealing with. While I was impressed with her flyer, I thought perhaps a slightly more conservative tone would better suit the corporate management audience I was targeting.

You can always tailor the marketing profile to show what you want. What is important is that it is an interesting concept and tool that you can try.

Lessons Learned:

- Create a marketing profile on yourself. It will help outline what you are looking for and your major skills and strengths.
- Tailor your marketing profile to how you want to market yourself. You are the product you are marketing.

Tool 7: Follow-Ups

It is important to follow-up with the aim to move the situation forward. Make notes after a call, interview, networking call, or meeting. Writing effective follow-up letters will be based on these notes.

Lessons Learned:

- When interviewing or networking, get a business card. This gives you the correct spelling of a person's name for thank-you notes, phone numbers, etc.
- Write the interviewer or contact as soon as possible after the meeting. Within forty-eight hours or less is a good guideline. As with the cover letter, try to keep it to one page.
- Express appreciation and restate how your qualifications best match the position's particular needs. Emphasize any areas you wish.
- Include any new information that might have occurred to you after the meeting or interview.
- Ask for or confirm any action or next steps to maintain progress.
- If you promised any references, provide them.
- Check for mistakes. Avoid using clichés. Make it look professional.
- Always send a thank-you note—even if you have been rejected for a job. It is courteous, and they might remember you for other future opportunities.
- When you have successfully landed a job, thank your friends and network for helping and supporting you along the way.

Tool 8: Tracking Forms

When I first started my job search, it was easy to mentally keep track of who I had spoken to, where I had applied, and what I had written in my cover letter. As time goes on, though, this gets harder.

Tracking forms were helpful for me. These can be simple spreadsheets or tables that you can develop to outline the pertinent details you wish to keep track of. I used a simple spreadsheet. For example, you can maintain a networking tracking form, showing whom you have contacted, when, a short description of what was said, and any follow-up or action items.

A job applications tracking form to track the positions you have applied for is especially useful. The job title, reference number, company, date applied, and follow-up steps are useful bits of information to maintain with records.

An interview tracking form can also be beneficial. Record the job title, reference number, company, date of interview, interviewer(s) name(s), brief notes on what transpired and follow-up interviews.

Lessons Learned:

- Tracking forms are very useful in a job search.
- A networking tracking form is useful to track whom you have contacted, when, and what was said. You might need to refer to them later.
- A job applications tracking form is useful to track the positions you have applied for and the statuses of each. The job title, reference number, company, date applied, and follow-up steps are good items to show.
- An interview tracking form is useful to track when and by whom you have been interviewed and what transpired. Record

the job title, reference number, company, date of interview, interviewer(s) name(s), brief notes on what transpired and follow-up interviews.

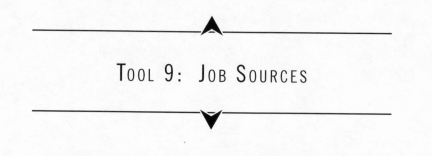

Tool 9: Job Sources

You can utilize several sources in your job search. These can be divided into four main categories, shown in order of success rate:

- Networking: personal and professional contacts, networking groups, industry/association groups, electronic professional networking sites (e.g. www.linkedin.com), chamber of commerce, board of trade.
- Recruiters: see www.directoryofrecruiters.com for a list of Canadian recruiters. You can also look in the Yellow Pages under employment agencies or personnel consultants.
- Internet: Workopolis, Monster.ca, careerbuilder.ca, ontario.ca/careers, gojobjobs.gov.ca, career sections of company websites.
- Direct Marketing: newspapers, publications, trade journals, research, etc.

More than half of jobs are found through networking. Being very independent, I hate to have to ask around and approach people. I would prefer to find a job posting and apply on my own, but I know that these methods are not as fruitful.

I found some interesting areas I had not considered by reviewing newspaper ads. Even if the job advertised is not suitable for you, perhaps the company is also hiring for other areas, and you can investigate further if you are interested in the company.

Recruiters are paid by the hiring employer to find them a suitable candidate. Avoid companies that ask you to pay a fee—and don't allow recruiters to send out your resume without your permission. It is recommended that you do not sign up with too many recruiters. Research them and settle on only one or two that you feel would best suit you. Be honest and up-front with them in your interview so that they are best equipped to find a good job match for you.

I spent a lot of time on the Internet looking at various job and company sites. You can put yourself on electronic career alert lists so that you are electronically notified by e-mail when a new job posting that matches your criteria comes up. This can save you time checking a particular site many times for new postings.

Utilize all the sources above. You never know which one could be the one that you land.

Lessons Learned:

- Job sources, in order of their success rate in obtaining one, are: networking, recruiters, Internet and direct marketing.
- Networking is the most successful method of landing a job. More than half of jobs are found through networking.
- If you use employment recruiters, research and use only one or two recruiters who best suit you.
- Avoid recruiters who ask you to pay a fee. They should be paid by the employing company.
- Don't allow recruiters to send out your resume without your permission. You want to be in control and knowledgeable as to who has seen your resume.
- Utilize electronic career alerts. By putting yourself on a company's automatic notification list, you can save yourself time.
- Research. There are many sources of job postings. Research and find out the sources that are available in your area.

NOTE FROM THE AUTHOR

When you are first downsized, you need to upsize yourself and get back on track. You say, "Okay, just pick yourself up and get another job." But it's not that easy sometimes. There are many books and articles on the mechanics of the how-to in job searching. I impart the various tools and lessons that I learned so you can upright yourself and land. But there are the memories that we will never forget: the moment when we realize we are being let go, the going home to tell our family, the change in life direction.

They say that life's challenges make you stronger. I know that I have learned and grown from it. Would I want to go through it again? No, but I know what to do now should it happen again. I have upsized myself after being downsized and have become a survivor now. I am moving forward now.

Upsizing yourself in a downsizing world is a skill that needs to be learned by many of us now. Lessons are learned through necessity as a result of downsizing being a reality of today's world.

Take heart with the stories that I have shared. Learn through the lessons that I have learned. You, too, will find your way.

God bless all the souls out there. All the souls who have ever been, are going through, or will be, downsized.

> May I be filled with loving kindness,
> May I be well,
> May I be peaceful and at ease,
> May I be happy.

—A Buddhist blessing taught by Linda, a wonderful yoga instructor at YMCA Camp Wanakita

My very best wishes to you.

Jeannette
Upsized Survivor in our Downsizing World

ENDNOTES

1. Career Transition Program, DBM publication, 2006.
2. "State Unemployment Insurance," United States Department of Labor, accessed August 29, 2010, http://www.dol.gov/dol/topic/unemployment-insurance/index.htm.
3. "State Unemployment Insurance Benefits," United States Department of Labor, accessed August 29, 2010, http://workforcesecurity.doleta.gov/unemploy/uifactsheet.
4. "Employment Insurance (EI) frequently asked questions: How long can I receive EI?" Service Canada, accessed September 6, 2010, http://www.servicecanada.gc.ca/eng/ei/faq/faq_general.shtml#How.
5. "Severance Pay," Ontario Ministry of Labour, accessed September 18, 2011, http://www.labour.gov.on.ca/english/es/pubs/guide/severance.php.
6. "Severance Pay," United States Department of Labor, accessed August 29, 2010, http://www.dol.gov/dol/topic/wages/severancepay.htm.
7. "Caught in the Time Crunch: Time Use, Leisure and Culture in Canada," *Canadian Index of Wellbeing*, June 15, 2010.
8. "Small business survival rates," SCORE, accessed September 6, 2010, www.score.org/small_biz_stats.html.
9. Rob Ferguson, "Economy nosedives; Critics demand action by Liberals as three months of falling output leave Ontario on road to recession," *Toronto Star*, July 4, 2008.
10. Noor Javed, "Historic observatory sold; University makes 'firm agreement with a buyer,' upsetting activists working to protect Dunlap site," *Toronto Star*, July 4, 2008.
11. Chris Sorensen, "Workers face turbulent skies," *Toronto Star*, July 4, 2010.
12. Tony Van Alphen, *Toronto Star*, July 3, 2008.
13. Business Section, *Toronto Star*, September 3, 2008.
14. Eckhart Tolle, *A New Earth* (New York: Penguin Group, 2006).

15. Randy Pausch, *The Last Lecture* (New York, New York: Hyperion, 2008).

16. Doris Day, "Que Sera, Sera (Whatever Will Be Will Be)," theme song to the television series *The Doris Day Show* (1967–73), 1956.

17. The Killers, "All These Things That I've Done," *Hot Fuss*, 2004.

18. "I've Got Soul, BUT I'm Not a Soldier," YouTube video, Nike Courage commercial, http://www.youtube.com/watch?v=-ae3tFI8wXE.

19. Mitch Potter, "America's problems converge," *Toronto Star*, July 30, 2010.

20. Rachel Beck, "CEOs paid more now than when economy was booming," *Toronto Star*, May 7, 2011.

21. Ibid.

22. Linda Barnard, "The Company Men," *Toronto Star*, January 21, 2011.

23. Chris Hedges, *Empire of Illusion* (Toronto, Ontario: Vintage Canada, 2010), 178.

24. Sandro Contenta, "Are they worth it?" *Toronto Star*, January 8, 2011.

25. Don Tapscott and Anthony Williams, *Wikinomics: How Mass Collaboration Changes Everything* (New York: Penguin Group, 2008).

26. *Merriam-Webster OnLine*, s.v. "wiki," accessed September 18, 2011, http://www.merriam-webster.com/dictionary/wiki.

27. Don Tapscott and Anthony Williams, *Macrowikinomics: Rebooting Business and the World* (Toronto, Ontario: Portfolio Penguin Canada, 2010).